Bars & Pubs

Fourth edition

Other Harden's titles

London Restaurants
UK Restaurant Guide
London Bars & Pubs
London for Free
Party, Conference & Event Guide

Interested in **eating** out in London too?

*Visit **www.hardens.com** for all your restaurant information. And you can sign up for free newsletters, and to take part in our annual restaurant survey.*

© Harden's Limited 2009

ISBN 978-1-873721-89-6

British Library Cataloguing-in-Publication data:
a catalogue record for this book is available from the British Library.

Printed and bound in Finland by WS Bookwell

Research Assistant: Rebecca Halfond
Production Assistant: Fiona Aranguren

Harden's Limited
14 Buckingham Street
London WC2N 6DF

CONTENTS

KEY

Traditional pub
(and/or beer a speciality)

Wine bar
(and/or wine a speciality)

Lounge bar
(and/or interesting range of cocktails or spirits)

Good Food

Gay
(includes Lesbian bars)

DJ

Live music

Dance floor
(dancing is also possible at many places just labelled 'DJ')

Outside tables
(excludes places with a few pavement tables)

Happy hours

Open late
(beyond midnight)

Telephone number – all numbers should be prefixed with '020' if dialling from outside the London area.

Map reference – shown immediately after the telephone number.

Website – the first entry in the small print.

Opening hours – unless otherwise stated, drinks are served seven days a week from 11am through to the normal statutory closing times (11pm, Mon-Sat; 10.30pm Sun).

Credit and debit cards – unless otherwise stated, Mastercard, Visa, Amex and Maestro are accepted.

Dress – where appropriate, the management's preferences concerning patrons' dress are given.

"Cover charge may apply" – this note appears where applicable.

FROM THE EDITORS

This is the fourth edition of our handy guide to drinking in London. And how the scene has improved since we published our first edition back in the mid-'90s! London has again asserted its rightful place at the centre of the drinking world.

The picture was not always so rosy. Even in the closing years of the last century, concepts such as lounge bars, DJs (in bars) and gastropubs were still either unknown or vanishingly rare. Even the cocktail bar – hardly a revolutionary concept, in the global scheme of things – was a beast rarely sighted in practice. And London's great legacy of Victorian (and earlier) boozers had only just begun (thanks, for once, to a benign change to the law) to shake off the 'dead hand' of big brewery ownership.

How different things seem now. London's very own concept, the gastropub – a word which only came into general currency less than a decade ago – has been such a success that it has been imitated in New York, and now in various other major cities of the USA. Perhaps even more remarkably, even in the Big Apple they now concede that London has become the world centre of cocktail 'mixology'.

Our aim with this book is a simple one: to help you find new and interesting places for a drink. Even more than is than is the case with restaurants, we suspect that whether you'll like a particular establishment or not is a function of your own age and circumstances. We've therefore not attempted any overall qualitative assessments, but rather an indication of the key features, and style, of each establishment which may – or may not – make it of interest to you personally. As with our restaurant guides, we've been anxious to do justice to the whole range of possibilities, from the most traditional inns and pubs, via wine and cocktail bars, to the slickest new style and lounge bars. With luck, this guide may even tempt you to try out of few establishments of a type which you wouldn't generally think of as being 'for you'!

If you like what you read and the places we lead you to – but more especially if you don't – we would like to hear from you. Please just send an email to mail@hardens.com headed "Bars and Pubs" with any feedback on existing reviews or suggestions for establishments worth including in the next edition.

Richard Harden   **Peter Harden**

DIRECTORY

The Abbeville SW4

67-69 Abbeville Rd   8675 2201   10–2D

In the backstreets of Clapham, this casual joint styles itself as a 'gastropub', but is more like a rambling, old-fashioned wine bar, that's been brought up-to-date. They make quite an effort on the food front here (even if results are a bit variable).
/ **Website:** www.theabbeville.com **Details:** Mon-Wed 11am-11pm, Thu-Sat 11am-midnight, Sun 11am-10.30pm. **Food:** Mon-Sat till 10.30pm, Sun til 9pm.

Absolut Ice Bar W1

31-33 Heddon St   7478 8910   3–2C

OK, you've got to do it once, haven't you? Kept at minus 5°C, this pay-to-enter bar, just off Regent Street, is (no, really!) made of ice from a Swedish river, as is everything within it. Don't worry about your thermals: they will lend you a "designer cape" to help keep you warm for your 40-minute visit slot. That, plus the (ice) glass of vodka, is all included in the price.
/ **Website:** www.belowzerolondon.com/icebar **Details:** Mon-Wed 3.30pm-11pm, Thu 3.30pm-11.45pm, Fri 3.30pm-12.30am, Sat 12.30pm-12.30am, Sun 3.30pm-10.15pm. **Food:** Wed-Sat 6pm-10.30pm. **DJ:** Sat night (times vary). **Cover charge may apply.**

Adlib SW10

246 Fulham Rd   7376 7775   5–3B

A good all-purpose plain-vanilla bar, light and spacious and decorated in Mediterranean style, located on Chelsea's so-called 'Beach'. On the drinks front, the house speciality is a good range of cocktails. / **Details:** Mon-Fri noon-midnight, Sat & Sun 5pm-midnight. **Food:** always available.

Admiral Codrington SW3

17 Mossop St   7581 0005   5–2C

You date yourself if you admit knowing that the 'Cod', as this Knightsbridge boozer was once known, used to be famous as 'Sloane Central'. Since the place had a major make-over in the late-'90s, its style is rather less traditional, and it's more of an all-purpose trendy hang-out, with a not-bad restaurant attached (where, on a sunny day, the roof retracts).
/ **Website:** www.theadmiralcodrington.co.uk **Details:** Mon-Thu 11.30am–midnight, Fri & Sat 11.30am-1am, Sun noon-10.30pm. **Food:** L only.

Ain't Nothing But W1

20 Kingly St   7287 0514   3–2C

*This battered-looking bar, near Carnaby Street, is one of the bizarrely few venues in town focussed on the blues, and being regularly packed out with devotees only adds to a general feeling of authenticity. Free entry too, for early birds – check website for details. / **Website:** www.aintnothinbut.co.uk*
Details: *Mon-Wed 6pm-1am, Thu 6pm-2am, F 5-3am, Sat 3-3am, Sun 3-midnight; no Amex.* ***Food:*** *always available.* ***Happy hour:*** *Mon-Fri 6pm-8pm, Sat & Sun 3pm-6pm.* ***Cover charge may apply.***

Akbar W1

77 Dean St   7437 2525   4–2A

*With its natural stone floors, leather armchairs and low tables, this Soho basement (below one of central London's priciest Indian restaurants) is aimed at the more mature end of the local media crowd – a smart and cosy sort of place, with an impressive range of spirits and exotic cocktails. / **Website:** www.redfort.co.uk/akbar* ***Details:*** *Mon-Sat 5pm-1am, closed Sun.* ***Food:*** *L till 2.15pm, D till 11.15pm.* ***DJ:*** *Fri & Sat.* ***Happy hour:*** *Mon-Sat 5pm-6pm.*

Al's EC1

11-13 Exmouth Mkt   7837 4821   9–1A

*This long-established canteen by the entrance to Exmouth Market is a diner by day and a bar by night (with DJs in the basement at the weekend until 2am). Arguably it's getting a little long in the tooth, nowadays, but its all-hours, something-for-everyone style still makes it a much-used local. / **Details:** Mon 8am-midnight, Tue-Fri 8am-2am, Sat 10am-2am, Sun 10am-11pm.* ***Food:*** *till 6pm, Fri & Sat till 9.30pm.* ***DJ:*** *Fri & Sat.*

Albannach WC2

66 Trafalgar Sq   7930 0066   2–3C

*A location as central as you could ever want makes this large, modern, Scottish-themed bar – with a pricey restaurant on the mezzanine level, complete with kilted waiters – a very handy West End rendezvous. Diners avoid the Fri & Sat entrance fee (after 10pm) for access to the attractive basement bar, Doon. There's some emphasis on cocktails, but malt whiskies, of course, are the star of the show (there are over 120 of them). / **Website:** www.albannach.co.uk* ***Details:*** *Mon-Sat noon-1am, closed Sun.* ***Food:*** *till 10pm.* ***DJ:*** *Thu-Sat (in Doon).* ***Cover charge may apply.***

The Albert SW1

52 Victoria St   7222 5577   2–4C

*For Victorian grandeur, few places beat this Westminster pub,
which – surrounded by faceless modern office blocks – conveys
the impression of a becalmed battleship of Empire.
Appropriately enough, as it is the only building in the locality
that wasn't blitzed. Downstairs, admire the original hand-
etched glass windows (1852) – upstairs there's ye olde carvery,
popular with MPs (there's a division bell) and tourists.*
/ Details: 11am-9pm. **Food:** always available.

The Albert NW1

11 Princess Rd   7722 1886   8–3B

*A mere stone's throw from Primrose Hill's two über-pubs
(the Engineer and the Lansdowne), this agreeable boozer
makes a more traditional and relaxed destination than its
trendy neighbours. Rather like the Engineer, it boasts a very
pleasant garden and decent food – the main difference is that,
on a sunny day, you might actually get a seat here!*
/ Food: Mon-Thu L noon-2.30pm, D 6.30pm-10pm, Fri L noon-3pm,
D 6.30pm-10pm, Sat & Sun all day.

The Albert & Pearl N1

181 Upper St   7354 9993   8–2D

*On the former site of the long-serving Medicine Bar (RIP),
this recently opened DJ bar has added a pretty, art nouveau
gloss to the existing interior to create a much plusher,
more 'grown up' destination. You could knock back beer,
but they also push the cocktails and champagne. Or perhaps
a bottle of Sauternes with homemade foie gras?*
/ Website: www.albertandpearl.com **Details:** Sun-Wed noon-midnight,
Thu noon-1am, Fri & Sat noon-3am. **Food:** till 10pm. **DJ:** weekends.
Cover charge may apply.

Albertine W12

1 Wood Ln   8743 9593   7–1C

*Founded long before its vast new neighbour Westfield was
a twinkle in the developer's eye, this simple Shepherd's Bush
wine bar remains a cosy and comforting low-key spot. There's
a fair selection of wines (most by the glass) written up on the
blackboards, and some nice, straightforward food too. Look out
for the occasional Beeb star – HQ is just up the road.*
/ Website: www.gonumber.com/albertine **Details:** Mon-Thu 11am-11pm,
Fri 11-midnight, Sat 6.30pm-midnight, closed Sun; no Amex. **Food:** till
10.30pm.

All Star Lanes

Victoria Hs, Bloomsbury Pl SW1   7025 2676   2–1D
95 Brick Ln E1   7426 9200   9–1D
Porchester Gdns W2   7313 8363   6–1C
Upmarket, retro-American bars (and diners) with bowling allies attached is proving a winning formula for central London's original bowling-party chain, which has spawned offshoots both in Bayswater, and in the East End. Perhaps it's not the trendiest format ever, but it's well-realised and certainly makes a change. / **Website:** *www.allstarlanes.co.uk.*

Alloro W1

19-20 Dover St   7495 4768   3–3C
For our money, one of the nicest cocktail bars in the West End, this attractive Mayfair venture shares its premises with a well-reputed Italian restaurant. The bar operation is entirely separate, though, and very popular with the locals for an after-work snifter. / **Website:** *www.alloro-restaurant.co.uk* **Details:** *Mon-Fri noon-10.30pm, Sat 7pm-10.30pm, closed Sun.* **Food:** *Mon-Fri noon-2.30pm.*

The Alma SW18

499 Old York Rd   8870 2537   10–2B
It's as a rugger-buggers' boozer that this popular Wandsworth institution is best known, but if you avoid match days you'll see that it's actually quite a fine Victorian Young's pub. Food is a big part of the operation, and there's a large dining area on the ground floor. / **Website:** *www.thealma.co.uk* **Details:** *Mon-Sat 11am-midnight, Sun noon-11pm.* **Food:** *till 10.30pm, Sun till 9pm.*

Alphabet W1

61-63 Beak St   7439 2190   3–2D
It was once an achingly hip hang-out, but this Soho 'oldie' (all things are relative) has weathered the passing of the years very well. It still hums at weekends, when there are DJs in the bar downstairs. The sofas in the window offer a prime vantage-point for watching the local media crowds go by.
/ **Website:** *www.alphabetbar.com* **Details:** *Mon-Sat noon-11pm, closed Sun.* **Food:** *till 9pm.* **DJ:** *Wed-Sat.*

Anam N1

3 Chapel Mkt   7278 1001   8–3D

*In a rather unlikely corner setting on Islington's (seedy) Chapel Market, a hip DJ bar with deeply '70s styling that's worth a visit. On the drinks front, cocktails — there's a long list — are the house speciality. / **Website:** www.anambar.com*
Details: Tue-Wed 6pm-midnight, Thu-Fri 6pm-2am, Sat 6pm-3am.
DJ: Thu-Sat. **Live music:** occasionally. **Happy hour:** Tue-Fri 6pm-8pm.
Cover charge may apply.

The Anchor SE1

34 Park St   7407 1577   9–3B

*With its big riverside terrace, this large Borough tavern is one of the best-placed central pubs at which to while away a summer's day (although it can feel rather touristy). The mainly 18th-century building was renovated a few years ago — seek out the smaller panelled rooms (often used for private events) for glimpses of its original period charm.
/ **Details:** Mon-Wed 11am-11pm, Thu-Sat 11am-midnight, Sun 11am-10.30pm. **Food:** noon-9.30pm.*

Anchor & Hope SE1

36 The Cut   7928 9898   9–4A

*This South Bank gastropub, near the Young Vic, has won a legendary reputation for its no-nonsense British grub (whose gutsy style is akin to the world-famous Smithfield restaurant St John). The main problem is that it's far too popular, and you may feel that hell will freeze over before it's your turn for a table (booking only for Sun lunch). At less frenzied times, it makes a pleasant, if quite basic, spot for a quiet pint.
/ **Details:** Mon 11am-11.30pm, Tue-Sat 11am-11.30pm, Sun 11am-5pm; no Amex. **Food:** L noon-2.30pm, D 6pm-10.30pm, Sun L noon-2pm.*

Anchor Tap SE1

20A Horselydown Ln   7403 4637   9–4D

*Hidden in the warren of streets behind Tower Bridge Road, this attractive wooden-fronted pub (the 'tap' of the former Courage brewery) offers an antidote to the trendy bars that have sprung up around Shad Thames. Sam Smith's beers and a games room off the main bar seem to attract a fairly mature local crowd, and there's a large terrace for warm days.
/ **Details:** Mon-Sat noon-11pm, Sun noon-10.30pm; no Amex. **Food:** till 9pm.*

Angel SE16

101 Bermondsey Wall East 7394 3214 11–2A
With fine views over the Pool of London, and Tower Bridge
in the distance, this nautically-themed Rotherhithe tavern
(now owned by Samuel Smith's) is worth bearing in mind when
you feel like a trip to the river. The building is merely 19th-
century, but the site is historic – almost 700 years old
(and mentioned by Pepys). / **Details:** noon-11pm; no Amex.
Food: noon-8pm, Sat & Sun noon-5pm.

The Angelic N1

57 Liverpool Rd 7278 8433 8–2C
It's easy to overdo the use of the word 'palatial' when it comes
to Victorian pubs, but it seems particularly appropriate when
applied to this tastefully updated Islington spot, which has been
made over into a very impressive and loungy modern boozer.
Food is a large part of the operation, and drinkswise the
emphasis is on wine and lager. Don't miss the grandiose
upstairs room. / **Website:** www.theangelic.co.uk **Details:** Sun-Thu
noon-midnight, Fri & Sat noon-1am. **Food:** till 10pm, Sun till 9.30pm.

Anglesea Arms SW7

15 Selwood Ter 7373 7960 5–2B
This early 19th-century freehouse must be one of the
most successful pubs in south west London – it certainly has
one of the most pukka locations (in the middle of a row
of white stucco houses in the heart of a South Kensington
residential street). Especially in warm weather, it's always
heaving with young locals, who – having filled up the small
paved garden – spill onto the pavement. The food, if without
any great pretensions, is pretty good too.
/ **Website:** www.capitalpubcompany.co.uk **Details:** Mon-Sat noon-11pm,
Sun noon-10.30pm. **Food:** L noon-3pm, D 6.30pm-10,pm, Sat & Sun
L noon-5pm, Sat D 6pm-10pm, Sun 6pm-9.30pm.

The Anglesea Arms W6

35 Wingate Rd 8749 1291 7–1B
One of the capital's first places to earn the description
'gastropub', this phenomenally popular destination – a short
stroll from Ravenscourt Park – is still one of the best. Fabulous
cooking is the main draw, but drinkers are by no means second-
class citizens, and the bare but characterful bar, with its real
fire and small terrace, attracts a lively crowd. There's a good
range of beers, quality wines, and seasonal tipples. / **Details:** no
Amex. **Food:** till 10.30pm.

Anise EC2

9 Devonshire Sq   7626 5000   9–2D
An impressive newcomer not far from Liverpool Street station – an Indian bar/restaurant that's an offshoot of Westminster's famous Cinnamon Club. The large and elegant bar has very much its own identity, and aspirations far beyond attracting off-duty City bankers. Small plates are available to complement a range of cocktails, beers and wines.
/ **Website:** www.cinnamon-kitchen.com **Details:** Mon-Fri 11am-midnight, Sat 6pm-midnight, closed Sun. **Food:** till midnight.

Annex 3 W1

6 Little Portland St   7631 0700   3–1C
You can't say they didn't 'go for it' on the design front, at this 'maximalist' hang-out near Broadcasting House, which is a sibling to the East End's Loungelover – no surface has been left undesigned. Food is a large part of the operation here – it's nothing special, but it does contribute to the place's overall charms as a Big Night Out destination. / **Website:** www.annex3.co.uk **Details:** Mon-Fri 5pm-midnight, Sat 6pm-midnight, closed Sun. **Food:** till 1 hour before closing.

The Antelope SW1

22 Eaton Ter   7824 8512   5–2D
Characterfully located on a side-street between Sloane and Eaton Squares, this late-18th-century pub benefits from a strong and very genuine atmosphere, and popularity is such that it can get very crowded. Despite the obvious 'heritage' charms, this is largely a tourist-free zone. / **Details:** closed Sun. **Food:** L noon-3pm, D 6pm-9pm, Thu & Fri 6pm-8.30pm, closed Sat D.

The Approach Tavern E2

47 Approach Rd   8980 2321   1–2D
This friendly pub, in a leafy side street, is one of the hidden delights of Bethnal Green. Bombed during WWII, it has been partly trendified in recent times – there's an art gallery upstairs, Czech beers on draught, and the patio is heated – but it retains some great features, including a jukebox filled with 'oldies'. The punters are a happy mix of locals, students, and staff from the nearby London Chest Hospital. / **Details:** Sun-Thu noon-11pm, Fri & Sat noon-midnight; no Amex. **Food:** L noon-2.30pm, Sat noon-4pm, D 6pm-9.30pm, Sun noon-4pm.

Aquasia Bar
Conrad Hotel SW10

Chelsea Harbour   7823 3000   5–4B

Can't get away to Monaco this weekend? Then a sunny-day trip to this luxurious (if rather anonymous) hotel overlooking Chelsea marina is about as close as London gets to the Riviera. Grab a spot outside for the best views of the water and yachts – otherwise there are floor-to-ceiling windows, by which you can sip a cocktail, or a glass of wine. A major refit is planned for mid-2009. / **Website:** *www.wyndham.com* **Details:** *10am-1am.* **Food:** *noon-11.45pm.* **Happy hour:** *Thu 6pm-8pm.*

Aragon House SW6

247 New King's Rd   7731 7313   10–1B

Overlooking Parson's Green, this attractive venue shares its imposing building with a branch of the British Legion. The ground-floor bar/restaurant has been decorated in a vaguely baronial style, and there's a further area downstairs. It's in the summer, though, that the beer garden and barbecue really come into their own. / **Website:** *www.aragonhouse.net* **Details:** *Mon-Fri 11am-11pm, Sat noon-11pm, Sun noon-10.30pm.* **Food:** *L noon-3pm, D 6 p,-10pm, Sat & Sun noon-9pm.*

Archduke Wine Bar SE1

Arch 153 Concert Hall Approach, Southbank
7928 9370   2–3D

Nightly jazz is a feature of this rambling fixture in railway arches by the South Bank Centre. It has been known for over a quarter of a century as a good option hereabouts for a drink before or after a concert (and now also for a steadying glass after a turn in the 'Eye'). The quality of the wines, however, far exceeds that of the food. / **Website:** *www.thearchduke.co.uk* **Details:** *Mon-Sat 8.30am-11pm, closed Sun.* **Food:** *till 10.45pm.*

The Arches NW6

7 Fairhazel Gdns   7624 1867   8–2A

This funny little wine bar of long standing has an obscure location on a Swiss Cottage side street, but locals seek it out nonetheless for its breakfasts (for which it has something of a 'name') and for its wine list – a curious-looking document, notable for its eclecticism and for offering some real 'finds'. / **Details:** *no Amex.* **Food:** *L till 3pm, Sun till 4pm, D till 10.30pm, Sun till 10pm.*

Argyll Arms W1

18 Argyll St   7734 6117   3–1C

The décor and scale of this grand pub, near the Palladium, make it, at least architecturally speaking, one of London's great Victorian boozers, with many wonderful original fittings. By day, it's the haunt of shoppers and local office-workers, but on Fri and Sat nights a younger crowd takes over. / **Details:** *Sun-Thu 10am-11.30pm Fri & Sat 10am-12.30am.* **Food:** *till 10pm.*

Artesian
Langham Hotel W1

1c Portland Pl   7636 1000   3–2C

Star restaurant/bar designer David Collins has done a magnificent job on his reworking of the bar of this grand hotel opposite Broadcasting House, which incorporates an eye-catching 'Chinese Chippendale' centrepiece into its glittering design scheme. If you want to 'put on the Ritz', so to speak, there are few better locations. Rums – a choice of 50 – a speciality. / **Website:** *www.artesian-bar.co.uk* **Details:** *10.30am-midnight.* **Food:** *always available.*

Artesian Well SW8

693 Wandsworth Rd   7627 3353   10–1C

Are you looking for "a fantasy nightclub and party venue created for indulgence in hedonistic pleasure"? If so, this lavishly-furnished ex-pub, spanning three floors, on the fringe of Clapham, might be just the job.
/ **Website:** *www.artesianwell.co.uk* **Details:** *Thu 5pm-3am, Fri & Sat 5pm-4am, closed Sun-Wed.* **DJ:** *Fri & Sat.* **Live music:** *Thu.* **Happy hour:** *Fri 5pm-7pm.* **Cover charge may apply.**

The Atlas SW6

16 Seagrave Rd   7385 9129   5–3A

Opposite a storage depot in the backstreets of Fulham (near Earl's Court 2), this ordinary-looking boozer had been made over into an incredibly popular gastropub, offering cooking in Mediterranean style. At meal times it fills up quickly, so get there early if it's either a quiet pint or a seat in the small garden that you're after. / **Website:** *www.theatlaspub.co.uk* **Details:** *Mon-Sat noon-11pm, Sun noon-10.30pm.* **Food:** *L till 3pm, D till 10.30pm.*

The Audley W1

41-43 Mount St   7499 1843   3–3A

*When the then Duke of Westminster was building this corner of Mayfair, he was determined that this pub should (in accordance with his wealth and status) be the grandest in the capital. The result is this opulent Victorian pile — all polished wood and gilded cornicing — which, to this day, remains one of the most impressive places in town in which to sink a pint. / **Food:** 11am-10pm, Sun noon-9pm.*

Auld Shillelagh N16

105 Stoke Newington Church St   7249 5951   1–1C

*This characterful Irish boozer, in Stoke Newington, is as 'traditional' an example of the type as you'll find in the Smoke. It's small but very friendly, serves a fine pint of Guinness and regularly plays host to live Irish bands. A loyal local fan club adds to the atmosphere. / **Website:** www.theauldshillelaghn16.com*

Aura SW1

48-49 St James St   7499 6655   3–3C

*Just off Piccadilly, a basement cocktail bar with an impressive design which, as they themselves describe it, offers "a rare mixture of extravagance and minimalism". It's half members' club/half bar nowadays, but before 9.30pm entrance is generally free to non-members. / **Website:** www.the-aura.com **Details:** call to check. **Food:** till 9.30pm. **DJ:** nightly. **Cover charge may apply.***

The Avalon SW12

16 Balham Hill   8675 8613   10–2C

*A recent refurbishment on the much-improving strip between Clapham and Balham, this large, extremely plushly converted pub benefits from some very swish outside tables (plus a lofty dining room on quite a scale). The food and wine 'offer' is impressive too, so it's no surprise the place has been an instant hit with the smarter locals. / **Website:** www.theavalonlondon.co.uk **Details:** Mon-Wed noon-11pm, Thu noon-midnight, Fri & Sat noon-1am, Sun noon-10.30pm. **Food:** Mon-Fri L till 3.30pm, D 6pm-10.30pm, Sat L noon-4pm, D 6pm-10.30pm, Sun till 9pm. **DJ:** Fri & Sat.*

The Avenue SW1

7-9 St James's St   7321 2111   3–4D

For an example of impressive '90s minimalism, you won't find better than this large St James's bar/restaurant. If you're looking for an all-purpose West End bar, it's still worthy of consideration, but don't go if you want quiet – with all those hard surfaces the decibel level can be deafening.
/ Website: www.danddlondon.com Details: Mon-Fri noon-11pm, Sat 5.45pm-11pm, closed Sun. Food: till 11pm.

Babalou SW2

The Crypt, St Matthew's, Brixton Hill   7738 3366   10–2D

St Matthew's Church dominates the heart of Brixton, and its crypt provides an impressive setting for this basement bar, now done out with North African design flourishes. It's a large space much used for events – parties (from two upwards) can reserve a kissing booth, a boudoir or, a more boring-sounding 'private area'. NB Sometimes open on Wed and Thu too.
/ Website: www.babalou.net Details: Fri & Sat 9pm-6am, closed Sun-Thu.
DJ: *Fri & Sat.* **Live music:** *varies-see website.* **Cover charge may apply.**

Babble W1

59 Berkeley Sq   7758 8255   3–3B

It's not the most upmarket venue in Mayfair – something to do with the Michael Jackson music often playing, perhaps – but this large bar, prominently situated at the south of the square, has quite a capacity, and boasts such features as a generous happy hour (5pm-7pm) and bookable basement booths – ideal for a party of up to 30 people. There's dancing too, mainly to the sounds of the '70s and '80s.
/ Website: www.babble-bar.co.uk Details: Mon-Wed noon-'late', Thu noon-1am, Fri noon-2am, Sat 6pm-3am, closed Sun. Food: always available. **DJ:** *Thu-Sat.* **Happy hour:** *5pm-7pm.* **Cover charge may apply.**

Babel SW11

3-7 Northcote Rd   7801 0043   10–2C

A lounge bar – one of the longer-running successes on Battersea's ever-popular 'strip' – with a light and elegantly-decorated interior. It's open-plan, though, so the noise of the crowd, lounging on sofas and pouffes, can get very loud.
/ Website: www.faucetinn.com Details: Mon-Thu 11am-midnight, Fri & Sat 11am-1am, Sun noon-12.30am. Food: till 10pm. DJ & Live music: Fri & Sat. **Cover charge may apply.**

Balham Bowls Club SW12

7-9 Ramsden Rd   8673 4700   10–2C

*Elderly bowls enthusiasts have been replaced by younger revellers at this club off Balham High Road, which is still decked out with the scoreboards and bowls paraphernalia of yesteryear. Nowadays run by the same group as Brixton's Dogstar, it makes a comfy and 'different' destination (and a good one if you fancy a game of snooker, £10). / **Website:** www.antic-ltd.com* **Details:** *Mon-Thu 4pm-11.30pm, Fri 4pm-midnight, Sat noon-midnight, Sun noon-11pm; no Amex.* **Food:** *Tue-Fri 6pm-9.30pm, Sat 1pm-9.30pm, Sun 1pm-5pm.*

Baltic SE1

74 Blackfriars Rd   7928 1111   9–4A

*A dramatic conversion of a one-time carriage factory, this Southwark bar/restaurant remains one of the better-known drinking destinations in town. On the booze front, vodka (over 30 types, with flavours from bison grass to caraway), killer cocktails and bottled beers are key. The restaurant at the rear is also fun. / **Website:** www.balticrestaurant.co.uk* **Details:** *noon-midnight.* **Food:** *bar snacks all day, L till 3pm, D till 11pm.*

Bam-Bou W1

1 Percy St   7323 9130   2–1C

*This four-floor townhouse bar/restaurant retains the bohemian air of old Fitzrovia, despite nowadays being part of the glamorous group which owns such stellar properties as the Ivy. Arguably the best bit is the opium-den style Red Bar, which makes a cosseting spot for a cocktail. (If you want food, there are snacks, or book for the pricey French-Vietnamese dining room.) / **Website:** www.bam-bou.co.uk* **Details:** *Mon-Sat 6pm-1am, closed Sun.* **Food:** *bar snacks.*

Bar 190 SW7

190 Queen's Gt   7584 6601   5–1B

*With its comfy leather sofas and panelled walls, this large and clubby room (entered off the lobby of a South Kensington hotel) is one of the few bars in town which manages to be both 'louche' and 'charming'. It's technically part of a club, and entry is sometimes restricted. / **Website:** www.gorehotel.com* **Details:** *noon-1am.* **Food:** *till 11.30pm.* **DJ:** *Fri & Sat.*

Bar Code W1

3-4 Archer St   7734 3342   3–2D

In a backstreet near Piccadilly Circus, this Soho bar manages the neat trick of being incredibly central, yet feeling something of a secret – just right for the gay scene at this dimly-lit cube of a room. Like its newer Vauxhall sibling, it has daily-changing theme nights. / **Website:** *www.bar-code.co.uk* **Details:** *4pm-1am.* **DJ:** *nightly.* **Happy hour:** *4pm-8pm.* **Cover charge may apply.**

Bar des Amis du Vin WC2

11-14 Hanover Pl   7379 3444   4–2D

Below Café des Amis, in a cute alleyway by the Royal Opera House, this cosy basement bar has long been a popular option for a pre-show glass of vino (there's a great selection), and perhaps a snack too – the cheese and charcuterie boards here are excellent. / **Website:** *www.cafedesamis.co.uk* **Details:** *Mon-Sat 11.30pm-1am, closed Sun.* **Food:** *till 11.30pm.*

Bar Du Musée SE10

17 Nelson Rd   8858 4710   1–3D

Once a tiny, narrow and dark little place, this handily-located bar has in recent years acquired an impressive rear extension giving on to a surprisingly elegant courtyard garden – especially worth knowing about if you're looking for a sunny days drink in the touristy heart of Greenwich. There's also a large restaurant (with summer barbecue) which, on a culinary basis at least, is hard to recommend. / **Website:** *www.bardumusee.com* **Details:** *Mon-Sat noon-1am, Sun noon-midnight; no Amex.* **Food:** *L Mon-Fri noon-5pm, Sat & Sun 11am-5pm, D Mon.*

Bar Estrela SW8

111-115 S Lambeth Rd   7793 1051   10–1D

Feel like a change of air? Head to Vauxhall's Little Portugal, and more specifically this bustling Portuguese café/bar – a relaxed and friendly place in which to sup a glass of beer, eat some tapas, and to watch the TV (if you speak the lingo). In the summer it can get very crowded, with the locals spilling out on to the pavement. / **Details:** *8am-midnight.* **Food:** *till 11pm.*

Bar Kick E1

127 Shoreditch High St   7739 8700   9–1D

This brightly-lit hang-out (an offshoot of Café Kick) occupies a still-unlovely stretch of Shoreditch High Street. It's regularly packed, however, with a wholesome twentysomething crowd, lured by an evening of table-footie. Half-time revivers come in the shape of beers and cocktails, plus Mediterranean fare in the café. / Website: www.cafekick.co.uk **Details:** *Mon-Wed 11am-11.30pm, Thu-Sat 11am-midnight, Sun noon-11.30pm.* **Food:** *L Mon-Fri noon-3, Sat-Sun noon-11pm (all day). D Mon-Wed 6pm-10pm, Thu & Fri 6pm-11pm .* **Happy hour:** *Mon-Sun 4pm-7pm.*

Bar Rumba W1

36 Shaftesbury Ave   7287 6933   3–3D

Live music most nights and a large dance floor remain at the heart of the appeal of this basement venue near the Trocadero, where Tue night Salsa classes are still a regular fixture. / Website: www.barrumba.co.uk **Details:** *Mon & Tue, Wed 8pm-3am, Thu & Fri 6pm-3.30am, Sat 9pm-4am, Sun 8pm-2am; no Amex.* **DJ:** *nightly.* **Happy hour:** *varies.* **Cover charge may apply.**

Bar Soho W1

23-25 Old Compton St   7439 0439   4–2A

With its big windows and its prime position on London's cruisiest street, this large 'n' loud heart-of-Soho establishment – half bar/half restaurant, and complete with glitter ball – is something of an out-of-towners' delight. But it also attracts quite a lot of locals, and is usually packed. / Website: www.barsoho.co.uk **Details:** *Mon-Thu noon-1am, Fri & Sat noon-3am, Sun 4pm-12.30am.* **Food:** *always available.* **DJ:** *Mon-Sun.* **Cover charge may apply.**

Bar Vinyl NW1

6 Inverness St   7482 5545   8–3B

The main claim to fame of this cool Camden Town outfit – which has survived since the late-'90s – is its record shop downstairs, where lovers of vinyl can browse to their hearts' content (and where some of the artistes themselves show up from time to time). The bar itself is modern, and offers a fair array of lagers and cocktails, as well as food. / Website: www.barvinyl.com **Details:** *Sun-Wed 11am-midnight, Thu-Sat 11am-1am; no Amex.* **Food:** *till 10pm.* **DJ:** *nightly.* **Happy hour:** *5pm-7pm.*

Bartique SW10

196-198 Fulham Rd   7351 1711   5–3B

Imagine the bar of a smart boutique hotel. Now take away the hotel. That's the impression given by this popular newcomer, which is as 'pure' a stand-alone cocktail bar as you're likely to find. If you want to nibble while you sip, sushi is available (brought in from a restaurant a few doors along Chelsea's so-called 'Beach'). / Website: www.bartique.co.uk Details: 5pm-1am. Food: till 10.30pm.

Bartok NW1

78-79 Chalk Farm Rd   7916 0595   8–2B

'London's only classical music bar', this Chalk Farm joint comes suitably decked out with velvet and chandeliers. (The music might also occasionally be traditional, Indian, or contemporary classical with "beat undernotes".) Hoegaarden and Stella are on tap, but wine and cocktails tend to be more the order of the day. / Details: Mon-Thu 5pm-1am, Fri 5pm-2am, Sat noon-2am, Sun noon-midnight; no Amex. DJ & Live music: varies. Cover charge may apply.

Beach Blanket Babylon

19-23 Bethnal Green Rd E1   7749 3540   9–1D
45 Ledbury Rd W11   7229 2907   6–1B

For stunning Gothic décor, you will struggle to find better places than this famous bar duo. The Notting Hill original (1991) was among London's earliest style bars, and – though it's been prettied up in recent years – retains much of its inimitable original style. The new offshoot (cum gallery) in Shoreditch is on an even more lavish scale. / Website: www.beachblanket.co.uk.

The Bear EC1

St John's Sq   7608 2117   9–1A

In an area progressively dominated by extremes, this bright, modern boozer, just off Clerkenwell Road (and overlooking historic St John's Gate), offers a refreshingly unpretentious alternative (and a pleasant terrace too). By night, you find the younger crowd upstairs, and the oldies below – the management suggests it has something to do with the stairs. / Website: www.thebearpub.com Details: Mon-Fri noon-11pm, Sat 6pm-11pm, closed Sun. Food: L till 3pm, D till 10pm. DJ: most Fridays.

The Bedford SW12

77 Bedford Hill   8682 8940   10–2D

A vast Victorian pile in Balham that once made Evening Standard pub of the year. You can use it as a regular, traditional pub (there are half a dozen ales on tap, plus fairly substantial food), but the place is a veritable entertainment palace, incorporating "Shakespeare's Globe" (a two-tier theatre) and a ballroom, and plays host to dance nights, comedy clubs, sports screenings and so on. / **Website:** *www.thebedford.co.uk* **Details:** *Mon-Thu 11am-midnight, Fri & Sat 11am-2am, Sun noon-midnight; no Amex.* **Food:** *L Mon-Fri noon-2.45pm, Sat noon-3.30pm, Sun noon-5pm. Dinner Mon-Fri 7pm-10pm, Sat 7pm-9pm, Sun 7pm-9.45pm.* **DJ:** *Fri & Sat, occasionally Sun.* **Live music:** *Mon-Thu.* **Cover charge may apply.**

Bedford and Strand WC2

1a, Bedford St   7836 3033   4–4D

Perhaps still of more interest for its excellent and reasonably priced selection of wines than its (improving) food, this Covent Garden basement is a handy destination for those looking for a quality wine bar. / **Website:** *www.bedford-strand.com* **Details:** *Mon-Fri noon-midnight, Sat 5pm-midnight, closed Sun.* **Food:** *L till 3pm D till 11.15pm.*

Bedroom Bar EC2

62 Rivington St   7613 5637   9–1D

For once, 'New York style' really does describe this cool bar — with its white-painted walls and iron pillars, it's a dead ringer for a downtown Manhattan loft. A good-looking crowd sips cocktails and bottled lager, and chats over the background of whatever the DJ is spinning — which could be lots of things. / **Details:** *Thu 7pm-midnight, Fri & Sat 7pm-2am, closed Sun-Wed; no Amex.* **DJ:** *Thu-Sat.* **Cover charge may apply.**

Bell EC4

29 Bush Ln   7929 7772   9–3C

"We believe it is the oldest small pub in the City of London", says a sign outside this boozer tucked away down the side of Cannon Street station. There was a time when the Square Mile was full of places like this, but it's quite a rarity nowadays (and non-traditionalists may find it on the cramped side). / **Details:** *Mon-Fri 11am-10pm, closed Sat & Sun.* **Food:** *noon-3pm.*

The Bell & Crown W4

11-13 Thames Rd   8994 4164   1–3A
*This popular Fullers pub is arguably the pick of the crop
in Strand-on-the-Green – a particularly picturesque part of the
Thames towpath near Kew Bridge with three neighbouring
pubs. If you're looking for classic traditional-boozer style,
you won't do much better than this one.* / **Details:** Mon-Sat
11am-11pm, Sun 11am-10.30pm. **Food:** L till 3pm, D till 10pm, Sun till 8pm.

The Belle Vue SW4

1 Clapham Common Southside   7498 9473   10–2D
*By Clapham Common tube, a bright stripped-down traditional
pub, which also makes a bit of effort on the food front. It's
a welcoming destination, and just a little removed from the
hurly-burly of the main drag.*
/ **Website:** www.capitalpubcompany.com/bellevue **Details:** Mon-Thu
11am-midnight, Fri & Sat 11am-1am, Sun noon-11pm; no Amex. **Food:** L till
2.30, D till 9.00pm, weekends noon-7pm. **DJ & Live music:** occasionally.

The Blue Bar
Berkeley Hotel SW1

Wilton Pl   7235 6000   5–1D
*When it opened, cliché-mongers had a field-day describing the
'ultra-cool' surroundings of the bar of this once rather stuffy
Knightsbridge hotel. David Collins's interior is indeed very chic
and – er – blue, and this is a comfy and perennially fashionable
(if extremely expensive) spot for a drink.*
/ **Website:** www.theberkeleyhotellondon.com **Details:** Mon-Sat 4pm-1am,
Sun 3pm-midnight. **Food:** always available.

The Betsey Trotwood EC1

56 Farringdon Rd   7253 4285   9–1A
*This triangular Shepherd Neame pub has an attractive,
scrubbed-up appearance, with décor blending original features
and modern touches. Expect to see a media-heavy crowd,
supping the brewery's bitters and seasonal ales (for example
Spring Hop), as well as lagers such as Hürlimann Sternbrau.
Lots of live music, mainly indie rock.* / **Website:** www.thebetsey.com
Details: 11am-11pm; no Amex. **Food:** L Mon-Fri noon-3pm, D 6pm-9pm.

The Big Chill Bar E1

Dray Walk, 91 Brick Ln   7392 9180   9–1D

Run by the annual festival of the same name, this capacious hang-out keeps a hippy vibe going throughout the year, offering a more mellow music selection than many other bars in the area. There's a large array of cocktails, wines and beers, plus simple food such as burgers and pizza. During the summer, bag a spot in the large seating area at the front.
/ **Website:** *www.bigchill.net/bar* **Details:** *Mon-Thu noon-midnight, Fri & Sat noon-1am, Sun 11am-midnight; no Amex.* **Food:** *Mon-Thu till 9pm, Fri-Sat till 8pm, Sun L 11am-6pm.* **DJ:** *varies - see website.*

Big Easy SW3

332-334 King's Rd   7352 4071   5–3C

If you're looking for an All-American experience in deepest Chelsea, you won't do much better than this well worn-in bar and 'crabshack'. Frozen margaritas are a speciality, and there is also a good range of US beers – the prices, though, might raise a few eyebrows in Boise, Idaho. Live bands plays '70s-onwards tunes nightly. / **Website:** *www.bigeasy.uk.com* **Details:** *Sun-Thu noon-11pm, Fri & Sat noon-midnight.* **Food:** *Sun-Thu noon-11pm, Fri & Sat noon-midnight.* **Happy hour:** *Mon noon-11pm, Tue-Fri 4pm-7.30pm.*

The Bishop's Finger EC1

Smithfield   7248 2341   9–2A

A place of pilgrimage for beer- and banger-lovers alike. This modernised Shepherd Neame pub (the company's original London venture) serves up a weekday feast of gourmet sausages (from Smithfield Market across the road), plus a range of their famous beers – choose from cask (Bishop's Finger, predictably, plus seasonal brews), keg (Masterbrew, Spitfire) or lager (Oranjeboom Pilsener). / **Website:** *www.shepherd-neame.co.uk* **Details:** *Mon-Fri 11am-11pm, closed Sat & Sun.* **Food:** *till 9pm.*

The Black Cap NW1

171 Camden High St   7485 0538   8–3B

This long-standing gay pub in Camden Town has recently fallen under new management. As Boyz magazine's 'best north London bar', they must be doing something right, but that's not all – this cabaret-pub is also the self-proclaimed 'Palladium of Drag'. Never a dull moment here!
/ **Website:** *www.theblackcap.com* **Details:** *Mon-Thu noon-2am, Fri & Sat noon-3am, Sun noon-1am.* **Food:** *till 10pm.* **DJ:** *nightly.*
Happy hour: *Mon-Wed .*

Black Lion NW6

274 Kilburn High Rd   7624 1424   1–2B

Amazing carving around the bar and an eye-catching gilded ceiling set the tone at this woody, warm and cosy Victorian boozer in Kilburn. Accommodation (around £40 per person per night) is also available. / Website: www.blacklionguesthouse.com **Details:** *Mon-Thu noon-midnight, Fri noon-1am, Sat 11am-1am, Sun 11am-11.30pm.* **Food:** *always available.*

The Blackfriar EC4

174 Queen Victoria St   7236 5474   9–3A

Their grammar's not up to much, but the management's claim that this Nicholson's boozer is "London's most unique public house" is not that far off the mark. It's the small building itself – constructed in 1916 and elaborately decorated in the art nouveau style (very rare, in the capital) – which makes it so special. Despite the volume of passing traffic, however, it's the large outside area which is the big deal for most City workers. / Website: www.mbplc.com **Details:** *Mon-Fri 11.30am-11pm, Sat 11am-11.30, Sun noon-10.30pm .* **Food:** *till 10pm.*

Bleeding Heart EC1

Bleeding Heart Yd, Greville St   7242 8238   9–2A

Long-time customers may still think of this intriguing warren (hidden-away north of Holborn) as a cosy wine bar, with a grander dining room attached. It's expanded like mad over the years, though, and – for those with drinking in mind – the most obvious destination these days is the highly popular tavern, where beer supplements the heavyweight French wine list. / Website: www.bleedingheart.co.uk **Details:** *Mon-Fri 7.30am-10.30pm, closed Sat & Sun.* **Food:** *till 10.30pm.* **Cover charge may apply.**

The Blind Beggar E1

337 Whitechapel Rd   7247 6195   1–2D

Notorious as the place where, in 1966, Ronnie Kray shot George Cornell, this otherwise rather standard East End boozer, opposite the Royal London Hospital, does boast one great non-historic attraction – a large, ivy-covered beer garden for summer. / Website: www.theblindbeggar.com **Details:** *Mon-Sat 11am-11pm, Sun noon-10.30pm.* **Food:** *Mon-Sat all day, Sun noon-6pm.*

Blue Posts W1

28 Rupert St   7437 1415   4–3A

Just your average, mild-mannered pub – or at least it would be if it wasn't slap bang in the middle of the West End. It's remarkable that this simply-decorated corner spot hasn't been Irish-themed or turned into yet another trendy bar. Perhaps it's because it's practically invisible – among all the flashing neon signs of Chinatown – that it's lasted so long. / **Details:** Mon-Thu 11am-11.30pm, Fri & Sat 11-Midnight, Sun noon-10.30pm. **Food:** till 9pm.

Bluebird SW3

350 Kings Rd   7559 1000   5–3C

This large and swanky D&D (the new name for Conran) outfit – comprising a restaurant, café and bar – occupies the characterful Chelsea landmark built in 1924 as "Europe's largest motor-car facility". The bar takes up quite a large part of the impressively airy first floor, and is a safer bet than the (overpriced) adjoining grill restaurant. / **Website:** www.danddlondon.com **Details:** Mon-Thu noon-midnight, Fri & Sat noon-1am, Sun noon-10.30pm. **Food:** L Mon-Fri till 2.30pm, Sat & Sun till 3.30pm, D Mon-Sat 6pm-10.30pm, Sun 6pm-9.30pm.

The Boathouse
Putney Wharf SW15

Brewhouse Ln   8789 0476   10–2B

It may have a snazzy modern building, but 'location, location and location' is what this Young's boozer is really all about. Its large riverside courtyard has quickly established itself as a key sunny-day Putney destination (and the bar can struggle to meet demand). / **Website:** www.boathouseputney.co.uk **Details:** noon-11pm. **Food:** Mon-Fri noon-10pm, Sat & Sun noon-5pm / 7pm-10pm.

Bohème Kitchen & Bar W1

19-21 Old Compton St   7734 5656   4–2A

A lounge bar/restaurant – from the same owners as the mega-successful Café Bohème next door – where similarly the food isn't bad at all. On sunny days, the (few) outdoor seats offer an excellent perch from which to watch Soho's weird and wonderful world go by. / **Website:** www.bohemekitchen.co.uk **Details:** Mon-Wed 10am-1am, Thu-Sat 10am-3am, Sun 10am-midnight. **Food:** Mon-Wed till midnight, Thu-Sat till 2.30am, Sun till 11pm. **DJ:** Fri, occasionally Sun.

Boisdale (Back Bar) SW1

15 Eccleston St   7730 6922   2–4B

*On the fringe of Belgravia, this rambling Scottish restaurant and bar – run by Scottish laird, Ranald Macdonald – is heaven for traditional types, offering a massive range of malt whiskies (250+), wines (400+, mainly claret) and cigars (100+). (You can smoke on the bookable terrace.) It's a comfy, clubby kind of place, but cool jazz adds to a lively atmosphere. You can also, at considerable cost, eat a dinner of fine, hearty fare here. / **Website:** www.boisdale.co.uk/belgravia **Details:** Mon-Fri noon–11pm, Sat 7pm–11pm, closed Sun. **Food:** till 10.45pm. **Cover charge may apply.***

Boisdale of Bishopsgate EC2

202 Bishopsgate   7283 1763   9–2D

*Down an alleyway next to Dirty Dick's, this characterful bar is an offshoot of the successful Belgravia bastion of traditional Scottish values. Its clubby charms have been pretty successfully re-created here for City gents, so lovers of claret and malt whisky are particularly well catered for. / **Website:** www.boisdale.co.uk/bishopsgate **Details:** Mon-Fri 11am–11pm, closed Sat & Sun. **Food:** till 9.30pm.*

Bond's Threadneedles EC2

5 Threadneedle St   7657 8088   9–2C

*Ten years ago, the idea of a place in the City that was half as stylish as this boutique hotel near Bank would have seemed pretty unlikely. Even these days, this venue with its airy (reclaimed banking hall) setting provides the kind of glamorous environment more traditionally associated with the West End. Adjacent, quite an ambitious – and pricey – business restaurant. / **Website:** www.theetoncollection.com **Details:** Mon-Fri 6.30am–11pm, Sat & Sun 7.30am–11am. **Food:** D till 10pm.*

Boogaloo N6

312 Archway Rd   8340 2928   1–1C

*They claim to have "the world's No 1 jukebox" (GQ Magazine), at this rock 'n' roll Highgate pub, which has hosted gigs from the odd big name, and where there's an active DJ and live events programme. Visit the website to check out the forthcoming line up. / **Website:** www.theboogaloo.co.uk **Details:** Mon-Wed 6pm–1am, Thu-Fri 6pm–2am, Sat 2pm–2am, Sun 2pm-midnight; no Amex. **DJ:** Thu-Sun. **Live music:** Sun.*

Booty's E14

92a Narrow St   7987 8343   11–1B

Until 1979, this low-ceilinged riverside spot (with impressive views) was part of premises that had been a boatyard since the 16th century. Nowadays, as a freehouse, they provide the setting for what looks like a plainly decorated wine bar, ornamented with black and white pictures recording the development of the Docklands. / **Details:** *Sun-Thu 11am-11pm, Fri & Sat 11am-midnight.* **Food:** *till 9.30pm.*

The Botanist SW1

7 Sloane Sq   7730 0077   5–2D

Don't we all muse on 'businesses we really wished we owned'? Well, this prominently-sited new bar/brasserie gets our vote. OK, the Martin Brothers (of 'Gun' etc fame) must have invested quite a lot in the elegant fitting out, but they've been rewarded with a pretty much constant full house/money machine since the day the place opened. Undoubtedly Sloane Square's best option for a drink – if you can find a perch, that is. / **Website:** *www.thebotanistonsloanesquare.com* **Details:** *Mon-Fri 8am-11.30pm, Sat & Sun 9am-11.30pm.* **Food:** *till 11.30pm.*

Le Bouchon Bordelais SW11

5-9 Battersea Rise   7738 0307   10–2C

The attractive Continental-style bar attached to this lively and long-established (est. 1986) Gallic restaurant has long been a popular destination in its own right. As you'd expect, most customers opt for Les Vins (more than 350 to choose from), but there is also a good selection of Les Bières, Les Cocktails and so on. / **Website:** *www.lebouchon.co.uk* **Details:** *Mon-Sat 10am-11.45pm, Sun 10am-10.30pm.* **Food:** *till 10.30pm, Sun till 10pm.*

The Boundary E2

2-4 Boundary St   7729 1051   9–1D

Sir Terence Conran's latest restaurant has not just a cafe and a small hotel attached, but also a comfortable and glamorous basement cocktail bar. Its hidden-away location, on the fringe of Shoreditch, and its low-key but impressive setting, give it quite a clubby feeling. For the moment, however, this is a club which anyone is free to join. / **Website:** *www.theboundary.co.uk* **Details:** *Mon-Fri noon-midnight, Sat 6pm-midnight, Sun noon-5pm.* **Food:** *L Tue-Fri noon-3pm, Sun noon-4pm, D Mon-Sat 6.30pm.*

The Bow Wine Vaults EC4

10 Bow Churchyard   7248 1121   9–2C

A particularly charming 'old City' location – in a pretty lane, under the impressive bulk of St Mary-le-Bow – contributes to the ambience of this traditional-style wine bar (which has a brasserie attached). It offers a good range of wines, reasonably priced. / **Website:** www.bowwinevaults.com **Details:** *closed Sat & Sun.* **Food:** *L till 3pm.* **Cover charge may apply.**

The Box WC2

32-34 Monmouth St   7240 5828   4–2B

Just by Theatreland's Seven Dials, this simple bar/café was one of the earliest wave of hip and gay (well, predominantly gay) bars to hit the centre of town, and it remains remarkably popular. They are not resting on their laurels, however, and booths have recently been installed to make socialising here a bit more intimate. A wide range of bottled beers and cocktails are served. Artwork changes monthly. / **Website:** www.boxbar.com **Details:** *11am-11pm; no Amex.* **Food:** *till 8pm.* **DJ:** *Thu-Sat.*

Bradley's Spanish Bar W1

42-44 Hanway St   7636 0359   4–1A

This curious destination – in a back alley near Tottenham Court Road tube – has been in the same ownership for over four decades. It boasts a tiny bar at street level, but (through a separate entrance) there's also a larger one below. Both attract a chilled, Bohemian crowd. The dark setting, with lots of little alcoves, gives a mainly Spanish impression, but the beers and lagers on offer are from multivarious sources. / **Details:** *Mon-Sat noon-11, Sun 3pm-10pm; no Amex.*

Bread & Roses SW4

68 Clapham Manor St   7498 1779   10–1D

It's nice to come across a boozer with personality, and this imposing trades union-owned Clapham gastropub certainly scores on that front. The drinks selection includes a special house ale, and there are a number of lagers on tap, but many drinkers go for wine. The attractive decked garden out back comes into its own for the African buffet Sun lunch. There are also regular DJ and music nights. / **Website:** www.breadandrosespub.com **Details:** *Mon-Thu 4pm-11.30pm, Fri & Sat noon-12.30am, Sun noon-11pm.* **Food:** *L till 3pm, D till 9.30pm.* **DJ:** *varies - see website.* **Live music:** *scheduled nights.* **Cover charge may apply.**

Brew Wharf SE1

Brew Wharf Yd, 1 Stoney St   7378 6601   9–4C

*The closest you'll get in London to the feel of your classic German Bierhalle, this South Bank venue has an atmospheric and very spacious setting, in a series of cathedral-like railway arches, near Borough Market. They even 'brew their own' and have 10 beers on tap, plus about 40 in bottles. There's also some pretty solid food to mop up the ale (plus a pleasant terrace). / **Website:** www.brewwharf.com **Details:** Mon-Sat 11am-11pm, Sun noon-6pm. **Food:** Mon-Sat L noon-3pm, D 6pm-10pm, Sun noon-6pm.*

Bricklayers Arms W1

31 Gresse St   7636 5593   4–1A

*This mock-Tudor inn (actually built in the 18th century) looks out of place in a quiet cut-through near Charlotte Street and is made more distinctive by the small lane that runs through an arch in the side of the building. It has a traditional and woody interior, and – as is typical for a Samuel Smith property – makes an ideal antidote for those for whom the area (which trendies describe as NoHo) is just a bit too hip nowadays. The Rolling Stones allegedly played their first gig here. / **Details:** no Amex. **Food:** L till 3pm, D till 8pm, Fri-Sun till 3pm.*

Bridge House SE1

218 Tower Bridge Rd   7407 5818   9–4D

*Adnams' range of beers is always quite a draw, so this boozer by Tower Bridge has a head start with real ale fans. From the outside, it looks like an old pub, but inside it's bright and airy. All the company's ales (including the seasonal brews) and their (impressive) wine list are available, and there's a dining room upstairs. / **Food:** always available.*

Brinkley's SW10

47 Hollywood Rd   7351 1683   5–3B

*If there is a 'Chelsea set' nowadays, this side-street bar/restaurant is its rallying point, and the place is frantically busy from early-evening onwards. It looks like a cocktail bar, but ownership by merchant John Brinkley means that the wine selection is actually the star attraction (and prices are notably reasonable). The rear restaurant has its charms, but the food is no great shakes. / **Website:** www.brinkleys.com **Details:** Mon-Fri 5pm-11.30pm, Sat noon-11pm, Sun noon-10.30pm. **Food:** till 11.30pm. **Happy hour:** 5pm-7pm.*

The Britannia W8

1 Allen St   7937 6905   5–1A

Always a superior boozer, this handy establishment, tucked–away just off Kensington High Street, was relaunched by Young's as a gastropub a couple of years ago. It comes complete with a conservatory, new fireplaces, and food that's not bad at all. / **Website:** www.britanniakensington.co.uk **Details:** Mon-Sat 11am-midnight, Sun 11am-11.30pm. **Food:** Mon-Sat 10.30am-10pm, Sun noon-9.30pm.

The Brown Dog SW13

28 Cross St   8392 2200   10–1A

A super-cute location – amidst the narrow Barnes lanes known as Little Chelsea (parking is a nightmare!) – adds to the appeal of this cosy and civilised pub, which was dolled up a couple of years ago. There's a small bar, although many of the tables are given over to eating, and the food here's a cut-above. Probably the best idea, especially in summer, is to head for the spacious walled garden. / **Website:** www.thebrowndog.co.uk **Details:** Mon-Sat noon-11.30pm, Sun noon-10.30pm. **Food:** till 10pm.

Buchan's SW11

62-64 Battersea Bridge Rd   7228 0888   5–4C

Just south of Battersea Bridge, this long-established, Scottish-themed wine (and whisky) bar has long been a key local haunt. There's a full-blown restaurant, or (good but quite pricey) bar snacks are also available. / **Website:** www.buchansrestaurant.co.uk **Details:** Mon-Fri noon-2.45pm & 5.30pm-10.45pm, Sat 12.30pm-3.30pm & 5.30pm-10.45pm, Sun 12.30pm-4pm & 7pm-10pm. **Food:** Mon-Sat 6.30pm-10.45pm, Sun 7-10pm. **Happy hour:** Mon-Fri 5.30pm-7pm.

Buddha Bar WC2

8 Victoria Embankment   3371 7777   2–2D

This offshoot of the famous Parisian venue, intriguingly located in a vast space newly 'discovered' under Waterloo Bridge, opened in 2008 to mixed reviews. With its low lighting, and giant Buddha statue, it's certainly a dramatic destination, however, and worth at least one visit to sample its pricey cocktails and bar snacks (and to soak up its trademark background beats). After 10pm, you need to be on the guest list. / **Website:** www.buddhabar-london.com **Details:** Mon-Fri noon-late, Sat 4pm-late, closed Sun. **Food:** L noon-3pm, D 5.30pm-1am (weekdays till 12.30am). **DJ:** nightly.

The Builders Arms SW3

13 Britten St   7349 9040   5–2C

A convenient location and a laid-back vibe have helped make this back street gastropub hugely popular, especially with younger Chelsea locals. Food is quite a large part of the operation, but this place makes a relaxed and comfortable destination whether you're eating or not.
/ Website: www.geronimo-inns.co.uk Details: no Amex. Food: L till 2.30pm, D till 10pm.

The Bull & Last NW5

168 Highgate Rd   7267 8955   8–2B

Rightly celebrated for its excellent food (and quickly famous after receiving a rave review in the Times), this Dartmouth Park pub is very popular all week long. To look at, though, it remains very much a classic Victorian boozer, and that is, of course, part of its charm. / Website: www.thebullandlast.co.uk Details: Mon-Thu noon-11pm, Fri & Sat noon-midnight, Sun noon-10.30pm; no Amex.
Food: Mon-Fri L till 3pm, D 6pm-10pm, Sat L noon-3.45pm, D 6pm-10pm, Sun L noon-3.45pm D 6pm-9.30pm.

Bull's Head SW13

373 Lonsdale Rd   8876 5241   10–1A

Nightly blues and jazz – it's one of the leading venues in town – is the top draw to this large Victorian Young's pub, near Barnes Bridge, whose rear music room is much grander than the norm for this kind of venue. Supporting attractions come in the form of a pleasant location near the Thames (though you don't see much of the river), a characterful bar and a cute backyard Thai bistro (The Stable).
/ Website: www.thebullshead.com Food: till 10.30pm.

The Bull's Head W4

15 Strand on the Grn   8994 1204   1–3A

This ancient and intriguingly rambling (Grade I listed) Chef & Brewer pub is on the Thames towpath, on the very pretty stretch downstream from Kew Bridge. The outside tables therefore have obvious attractions. The interior has had an attractive, if slightly suburban, refit. Befitting the style, wine is a popular choice of tipple, but there are also half a dozen lagers and bitters on tap. / Food: till 10pm.

Bünker WC2

41 Earlham St   7240 0606   4–2C

*On a north-Covent Garden site, the premises originally
launched as the Freedom Brewing Company maintain the
microbrewery tradition. The aim nowadays is to re-create
a German Bierhalle, although the end result is still rather
industrial in feel. As well as the house brews, there are also
cocktails (plus simple food).* / **Website:** *www.bunkerbar.com*
Details: *Mon-Wed noon-11pm, Thu noon-11.30pm, Fri & Sat noon-midnight,
Sun noon-10.30pm.* **Food:** *till 10pm.* **DJ:** *Thu-Sat.*

Cactus Blue SW3

86 Fulham Rd   7823 7858   5–2C

*Even after a good few years in business, the modernistic design
of this Chelsea bar/restaurant can still seem impressive,
certainly for this part of town. The place is owned by the
Maxwell's burgers chain, and the 'Pacific Rim' food on offer is a
less reliable attraction than a few drinks in the bar.*
/ **Website:** *www.cactusblue.co.uk* **Details:** *Mon-Sat 5pm-midnight,
Sun 4pm-11.30pm.* **Food:** *D till 11pm.* **Happy hour:** *5.30pm-8.30pm.*

Cafe 1001 E1

Dray Walk, 91 Brick Ln   7247 9679   9–1D

*By day it lives up to its café moniker (with an amazing array
of fresh salads and sarnies), but, as the evening draws in,
this bohemian East End joint becomes a bar. Music (live on
Wed) starts playing, and they open up the warehouse-style
room, with its worn sofas and dance floor, to the rear.
In summer, the courtyard – with a dozen picnic tables and
a barbecue – comes into its own. Drink beer or cider
(all bottled or canned).* / **Website:** *www.cafe1001.co.uk*
Details: *6am-midnight; no Amex.* **DJ:** *nightly.* **Live music:** *Wed evening.*

Café Bohème W1

13 Old Compton St   7734 0623   4–2A

*A phenomenal success story, this corner-site cafe-bar-
restaurant, recently totally refurbished, remains a buzzing
linchpin of Soho life. It's Continental in style – you can get
anything from a coffee or (from 11pm) a beer to a full-blown
Gallic bistro meal at pretty much any time of day, and much
of the night.* / **Website:** *www.cafeboheme.co.uk* **Details:** *Mon-Fri
7.30am-3am, Sat 8am-3am Sun 8am-midnight.* **Food:** *Mon-Sat till 2.30am,
Sun till 11.30pm.* **Cover charge may apply.**

Café Kick EC1

43 Exmouth Mkt 7837 8077 9–1A

No prizes for guessing that football is what this tiny, shack-like café-bar is all about – there are a number of Fussball tables, and the décor and the TV are devoted to the Beautiful Game. With outside tables, food served tapas-style and a boho Exmouth Market location, the atmosphere is distinctly Continental. There is also has a Shoreditch sibling, Bar Kick. / **Website:** www.cafekick.co.uk **Details:** Mon-Thu noon-11pm, Fri & Sat noon-midnight, closed Sun in winter. **Food:** till 10pm. **Happy hour:** 4pm-7pm.

Cafe Sol SW4

56 Clapham High St 7498 8558 10–2D

If you're under 25 and out on the pull, this raucous Clapham Mexican bar/café may well be the place for you. You can party on till late too. / **Website:** www.cafesol.net **Details:** Sun-Thu 12.30pm-2am, Fri & Sat 12.30-3am. **Food:** Sun-Thu till 11.45pm, Fri-Sun till 12.45pm. **DJ:** Fri & Sat.

Callooh Callay EC2

65 Rivington St 7739 4781 9–1D

You go through a huge wardrobe to get to the main section of the bar at this zany early-2009 Shoreditch newcomer – doubtless you've already spotted the reference to Lewis Carroll's 'Jabberwocky' in the name. Run by an ex-manager of Loungelover, it looks set to occupy a similarly swish niche in the local scene. / **Website:** www.calloohcallaybar.com **Details:** Sun-Wed 5pm-11pm, Thu noon-11pm, Fri & Sat 6pm-1am; no Amex. **Food:** till 11pm. **DJ:** Fri & Sat.

The Calthorpe Arms WC1

252 Grays Inn Rd 7278 4732 9–1A

King's Cross may be up-and-coming, but the area near the station itself still has its seedy side, and this welcoming traditional pub has long been one of the better stopping-off points nearby. As well as the usual Young's brews, guest beers are regularly featured: CAMRA awards testify to the care taken in looking after them. / **Website:** www.youngs.co.uk **Details:** Mon-Thu, Sun 11am-11pm, Fri & Sat 11am-midnight, ; no Amex. **Food:** L till 2.30pm, D till 9.30pm.

The Camden Head N1

2 Camden Walk   7359 0851   8–3D

*This high Victorian pub – with its impressive glass and roaring (coal-effect) fires – is rather confusingly named, as it is in fact in the heart of Islington's quiet backstreets, near the antiques market. Attractions include a comedy club nightly (except Tue) and a pleasant sunny-day terrace. / **Details:** Sun-Tue 11am-11pm, Wed-Thu 11am-midnight, Fri & Sat 11am-1am. **Food:** till 8pm.*
Cover charge may apply.

Camino N1

3 Varnishers Yd   7841 7331   8–3C

*A sign of the way things are going around King's Cross – this smart Spanish bar-cum-restaurant has been quite a success (including being voted bar of the year by The Observer). True to stereotype, the atmosphere by night is often vibrant, and the tapas and vino are good too. / **Website:** www.camino.uk.com
Details: Mon-Wed noon-midnight, Thu-Sat noon-1am, Sun 11am-11pm.
Food: tapas till 11pm. **DJ:** Thu-Sat. **Live music:** varies.*

Cantaloupe EC2

35-42 Charlotte Rd   7729 5566   9–1D

*This industrial-chic bar/restaurant almost single-handedly put Shoreditch on the map, and, although no longer cutting-edge cool, is still often packed with a wide variety of punters. No cocktails, but just about every sort of alcohol is available, and there are good tapas-style snacks (plus Sun brunch). / **Website:** www.cantaloupe.co.uk **Details:** Mon-Fri noon-4pm, 6pm-11pm, Sat 6pm-11pm. **Food:** till 10.30pm. **DJ:** Fri & Sat.*

The Captain Kidd E1

108 Wapping High St   7480 5759   11–1A

*This Wapping riverside tavern is named after a famous pirate who was hanged nearby, and looks every bit an ancient inn (complete with a cute courtyard entrance). It was in fact a warehouse until a few years ago when it was converted by brewers, Sam Smith's. Nowadays, it has two bars, and an independently-run restaurant upstairs ('The Gallows'). / **Food:** noon-2.45pm, 6.30pm-9.45pm.*

Cardinal SW1

23 Francis St 7834 7260 2–4B

Samuel Smith's refurbishment of recent years really could have made much more of this corner boozer, hidden-away behind Westminster Cathedral (and whose style of late-Victorian architecture it emulates). A soaringly elegant building, it deserves to be developed into some sort of 'destination'. / **Food:** L till 3pm, D till 9pm.

Cargo EC2

83 Rivington St 7739 3440 9–1D

Former railway arches provide a perfect industrial-look setting for what, as the queues attest, remains one of Shoreditch's foremost scenes. The restaurant (with terrace) and bar each have their own arches, separate from that containing the entertainment, but the same entrance fee applies whichever your chosen way in. / **Website:** www.cargo-london.com **Details:** Mon-Thu 6pm-1am, Fri & Sat 6pm-3am, Sun 6pm-midnight; no Amex. **Food:** always available. **DJ:** nightly. **Cover charge may apply.**

The Carpenter's Arms E2

73 Cheshire St 7739 6342 9–1D

This East End boozer has its claim to historical fame in having once been owned by the Kray family. It's been dolled up, somewhat, of late (and even does food nowadays), but it's the splendid range of beers (mostly bottled) which made it fancyapint.com's Best Newcomer 2008. / **Website:** www.carpentersarmsfreehouse.com **Details:** Sun-Thu noon-11.30pm, Fri & Sat noon-12.30am; no Amex. **Food:** till 5pm, bar snacks till 10pm.

The Castle W11

100 Holland Park Ave 7313 9301 6–2A

This prominently-located boozer has long been a local landmark, near Holland Park tube. After a sophisticated makeover a few years ago, its funky style puts it more in the lounge-bar category nowadays, and – though it's far from being a typical gastropub – food is now quite a large part of the operation. / **Details:** noon-midnight. **Food:** Mon-Fri L till 3pm, D 5pm-10pm, Sat & Sun 10am-10pm.

Cat & Mutton E8

76 Broadway Mkt 7254 5599 1–2D

If the East End is the new frontier, this Hackney gastropub was one of the earlier pioneers. When it comes to the décor, they seem to have done a lot of stripping-out and not much putting-in, but the place has managed to pull in a strong local following nonetheless. Indeed, in spring 2009, they're opening an offshoot nearby, called London Fields.
/ **Website:** www.catandmutton.co.uk **Details:** Mon 5.30pm-11pm, Tue-Sat noon-11pm, Sun noon-10.30pm. **DJ:** Sun.

Catch E2

22 Kingsland Rd 7729 6097 9–1D

At this cool two-level bar, in the ever more trendy Shoreditch strip, you can while away the time over a game of pool. If you prefer to concentrate on drinking (mostly draught lager), however, seek out one of the US-style booths at the front. DJs and up-and-coming live acts also feature regularly.
/ **Website:** www.thecatchbar.com **Details:** Tue & Wed 6pm-midnight, Thu-Sat 6pm-2am, Sun 7pm-1am, closed Mon. **DJ:** nightly. **Live music:** varies-see website.

Cecconi's W1

5A Burlington Gdns 7434 1500 3–3C

A couple of blocks from Savile Row, this Italian corner brasserie (owned by Soho House) is one of Mayfair's most thriving success stories, and is packed all hours of the day with a chic crowd. You too can join in the fun for no more than the price of a cocktail, or a glass of prosecco (and you also can snack here on 'Chichetti' – Italian tapas – or have a pricey full meal).
/ **Website:** www.cecconis.co.uk **Details:** Mon-Fri 7am-11.30pm, Sat 8am-11.30pm Sun 8am-10.30pm. **Food:** Mon-Sat 7am-midnight, Sun 8am-11pm. **Cover charge may apply.**

Cellar Gascon EC1

59 West Smithfield 7600 7561 9–2B

One for wine-aficionados and gastronomes – this buzzing cellar is the budget (but not exactly cheap!) spin-off from the famous Club Gascon, next door, offering a particularly good selection of wines from south west France. If you want to eat, don't take a veggie: the place is known for tapas-style dishes laden with foie-gras. / **Website:** www.cellargascon.com **Details:** Mon-Fri noon-midnight, closed Sat & Sun. **Food:** till 11.30pm.

The Chandos WC2

29 St Martin's Ln   7836 1401   2–2C

Just off Trafalgar Square, this large, rambling corner pub owned by Samuel Smiths has long been known as a handy West End rendezvous. It has recently come under new management but its 'Brief Encounter' charm remain essentially the same as ever.
/ **Food:** till 7pm, Fri-Sun till 6pm.

The Chapel NW1

48 Chapel St   7402 9220   6–1D

Near Edgware Road tube, this was one of the earlier-wave places to jump on what's subsequently become the gastropub bandwagon, and still does what it does well. Unusually for such a central pub, it has a small garden and terrace.
/ **Details:** noon-11pm. **Food:** L till 2.30pm, D till 10pm.

Chapel Bar N1

29a Penton St   7833 4090   8–3D

A large, low-ceilinged Islington bar, which – despite being slightly off the main drag – has shown a lot of staying power over what is now nearly a decade in business. Every day sees a different DJ, comedy night or open-mic session (varying charges apply).
/ **Website:** www.thechapelbar.co.uk **Details:** Mon-Thu 5pm-1am, Fri & Sat noon-3am, Sun noon-midnight. **Food:** till 10pm, excluding Sun. **DJ:** varies - see website. **Live music:** varies-see website. **Happy hour:** Mon-Wed 5pm-8pm, Thu-Sat 5pm-7pm.

The Charles Lamb N1

16 Elia St   7837 5040   8–3D

It's worth truffling out this tucked-away pub in the cute backstreets near Angel. In a blow to our national pride, the French owners rather irritatingly do the classic gastropub formula very well indeed, with good-value (yes, French) food, and excellent wine, and also a carefully chosen range of native beers (many on draught), ciders and perries.
/ **Website:** www.thecharleslambpub.com **Details:** Mon & Tue 4pm-11pm, Wed-Sun noon-11pm; no Amex. **Food:** Wed-Sat noon-3pm, Mon-Sat 6pm-9.30pm, Sun 12-6pm.

China Tang
The Dorchester W1

Park Ln   7629 9988   3–3A

David Tang's opulent, Shanghai-in-the-30's cocktail bar, in the basement of the Dorchester, is one of the most glamorous in town (and much preferable to the hotel's own bars upstairs). It's sometimes surprisingly quiet, and ideal for a relaxed drink. If you have money to burn, you can dine afterwards in the super-swanky adjacent restaurant. / Website: www.thedorchester.com
Details: *11am-midnight.* **Food:** *Mon-Fri L till 3.30pm, Sat & Sun L till 4pm, Mon-Sun D till midnight.*

Churchill Arms W8

119 Kensington Church St   7727 4242   6–2B

The renown of this Fullers hostelry a couple of minutes' walk from Notting Hill Gate has little to do with the beer (though it is good) or the landlord (who is a character). At the back of the rather ordinary bar, a pretty and airy conservatory is to be found, whose amazing and very cheap Thai food is a west London legend. Oddly for a pub, you can book — a good idea, as it's always rammed full. / Website: www.fullers.co.uk
Details: *Sun-Wed 11am-11pm, Thu-Sat 11am-midnight, Sun noon-10.30pm.* **Food:** *till 10pm.*

Cicada EC1

132-136 St John St   7608 1550   9–1A

Will Ricker's funky bar/restaurant is perennially packed with a trendy local crowd. The quality oriental food on offer is an attraction in its own right, and there's also a good cocktail list. The Red Room downstairs (usually available only for private hire) is decorated in an opulent, 'opium den' style that's strikingly at odds with the concrete bar and leather banquettes above. / Website: www.rickerrestaurants.com **Details:** *Mon-Fri noon-11pm, Sat noon-late.* **Food:** *till 10pm.*

The Cinnamon Club SW1

30-32 Great Smith St   7222 2555   2–4C

The area around Westminster Abbey not being exactly 'jumping', so it's a surprise to find this former library nowadays transformed into a successful Indian restaurant, with a surprisingly groovy basement bar that goes on till late. Or for a civilised cocktail, try the comfy ground-floor bar (which really is furnished with books). / Website: www.cinnamonclub.com
Details: *Mon-Sat 11am-11.45pm, closed Sun.* **Food:** *till 11pm.*

The Cittie of Yorke WC1

22 High Holborn 7242 7670 9–2A

Complete with large overhead wine butts, wooden booths and a vaulted ceiling, this cavernous Samuel Smiths tavern, next to Gray's Inn, is perhaps better endowed with historical fixtures and fittings than any other pub in London. It's certainly an atmospheric watering hole, if not an especially cosy one. / **Details:** *closed Sun.* **Food:** *till 9.30pm.*

City Limits E1

16-18 Brushfield St 7377 9877 9–2D

Once outside the City proper, but now engulfed by the expansion of the money-factories and the trendification of Spitalfields, this family-owned joint offers a welcome island of consistency in a fast-evolving part of town. Despite refurbishment a couple of years ago, the general style is still very much (champagne and) wine-bar-circa-1984, and the long-serving chef still cooks in the restaurant downstairs. / **Website:** *www.citylimits-winebar.co.uk* **Food:** *L till 3pm, D till 9pm.*

The Clachan W1

34 Kingly St 7494 0834 3–2C

Proximity to Liberty's department store ups the tone at this tucked-away Nicholson's pub (which, in days past, was actually owned and run by the shop). Its interior still has a number of period features – the pub opened in 1823 – which helps to make this a more-than-usually civilised retreat from the West End. / **Food:** *till 10pm.*

Claridges Bar
Claridges W1

55 Brook St 7629 8860 3–2B

This famed hotel threw off its staid image a few years back when it emerged from a no-expense-spared revamp. And nowhere is this more obvious than in its sleekly glamorous, Deco-style cocktail bar, notable for its cosmopolitan buzz. / **Website:** *www.theclaridgeshotellondon.com* **Details:** *Mon-Sat noon-1am, Sun noon-midnight.* **Food:** *Mon-Sat till midnight, Sun till 11pm.*

The Clifton Hotel NW8

96 Clifton Hill   7372 3427   8–3A

Is this the most genteel pub in London? Discreetly located in the middle of a street of grand St John's Wood houses, it has the most modest of signs and a location that seems to have been chosen to avoid anything so vulgar as passing trade. (Perhaps this is why Edward VII is reputed to have conducted his liaison with Lillie Langtry here.) Its charming interior makes it well worth seeking out, and there's also a pretty terrace.
/ **Website:** www.cliftonstjohnswood.com **Details:** Mon-Sat noon-11pm, Sun noon-10.30pm. **Food:** till 9.30pm.

The Clissold Arms N2

115 Fortis Gn   8444 4224   1–1C

Music anoraks may recall that this pub on the East Finchley/Muswell Hill border is linked with the glory days of The Kinks. You could accuse its recent 'gastro' makeover of looking a bit Identikit, but the modern panelled interior undoubtedly creates a relaxed atmosphere, and other plus points include good victuals and drinks, and a large amount of outside space. / **Details:** Mon-Thu noon-11pm, Fri & Sat noon-midnight, Sun noon-10.30pm. **Food:** Mon-Sat L noon-4.30pm, D 6pm-10pm, Sun noon-9pm.

The Coach & Horses SE10

13 The Mkt, Greenwich   8293 0880   1–3D

On the southern corner of Greenwich's charming covered market (and with a large, heated terrace in the market itself), this understated modern pub is predictably mobbed at weekends. An open fire adds to its charms at any time.
/ **Details:** Mon-Fri noon-11pm, Sat 11pm-midnight, Sun 11pm-10.30pm; no Amex. **Food:** noon-8pm.

The Coach & Horses W1

29 Greek St   7437 5920   4–3A

The fame of this Soho pub is boosted both by its journalistic associations (the staff of Private Eye having held a fortnightly lunch in its upstairs room since the paper was founded). It's typically a packed watering hole, whose battered, pinkly-lit décor has changed little since the war, and attracts a diverse clientele. / **Details:** no Amex. **Food:** always available.
Happy hour: Mon-Thu till 4pm.

Coach & Horses EC1

26-28 Ray St   7278 8990   9–1A

A smart but otherwise unremarkable-looking boozer, not far from Hatton Garden. It's worth seeking out for simple but above-average nosh, and also makes a civilised place for a pint, or a reasonably-priced bottle of vino.
/ **Website:** www.thecoachandhorses.com **Details:** Sat 6pm-11pm, Sun noon-3pm, Mon-Fri noon-11pm. **Food:** till 10pm.

The Coal Hole WC2

91 Strand   7379 9883   2–2D

This large, high-ceilinged Nicholson's ale house is a long-established stand-by for a Theatreland drink, and draws a diverse crowd. Mock-Tudor styling may not be all the rage nowadays, but here it works surprisingly well. Downstairs, there is also a cosier basement bar. / **Details:** Tue-Sat 10am-midnight, Sun & Mon 10am-11pm. **Food:** till 10pm.

Coburg Bar
The Connaught W1

Carlos Pl   7499 7070   3–3B

Time Out's best bar of 2008, the chic (Parisienne-designed) bar of this relaunched Mayfair hotel – in its former incarnation, a famously crusty sort of place – still manages to be something of a secret hide-away at the rear of the building. Cocktails are the thing, and whiskies – with some 75 in stock – a speciality.
/ **Website:** www.the-connaught.co.uk **Details:** 11am-11pm. **Food:** always available.

Cock Tavern EC1

East Poultry Ave, Central Markets   7248 2918   9–2A

One of the few London pubs with a licence permitting ale to be served from dawn (for Smithfield meat-traders), this long-established cellar spot is literally under the market. Breakfasts (and also lunch) are a feature and, as you might hope, fry-ups are the speciality. The setting has a certain homely charm, but the décor would win few prizes for style. / **Details:** Mon-Fri 6am-3pm, closed Sat & Sun. **Food:** B till 10.30am, L till 2.30pm.

Cockpit EC4

7 St Andrews Hill   7248 7315   9–2B
This funny little freehouse – in the City's back lanes, near Cannon Street station – was the venue for the last legal cock fight in the Square Mile, and the sign over its door is one of the few reminders of what was once a popular mass-entertainment. This is the sort of unchanging local they just don't make any more – anyone for a game of shove ha'penny? / Details: no Amex. Food: L till 2.30pm.

Coco Momo W1

79 Marylebone High St   7486 5746   2–1A
A former boozer on a Marylebone corner has been transformed into this attractive joint, which styles itself as a 'café/bar'. The overall look is arguably slightly anonymous, but this is still a handy place to know about in a part of town still short on airy, modern drinking spaces. / Website: www.cocomomo.co.uk Details: Mon-Thu 10am-11pm, Fri 10am-midnight, Sat 9am-midnight, Sun 9am-10.30pm. Food: till 5pm.

Cocoon W1

65 Regent St   7494 7600   3–3D
It may be oddly laid out in a series of 'pods', but this first-floor West End venture (from the Eclipse bar people) benefits from 'film set' looks and has proved an enduring hit over a number of years, with a rather beautiful crowd. It's a handy late-evening venue too, with good-quality (if pricey) oriental fare available till 1am. / Website: www.cocoon-restaurants.com Details: Mon-Fri noon-3pm & 5.30pm-1am, Sat 5.30pm-3am, Thu-Sat 11pm-3am . Food: till 1am. DJ: Thu-Sat.

The Collection SW3

264 Brompton Rd   7225 1212   5–2C
The truly impressive space – reached by a catwalk designed by Lord Foster, no less – helps make this popular Eurotrash/fashion world hang-out an ongoing success (both as a bar and as a venue for private events). There's a mezzanine restaurant too, but it's only really of interest as a vantage point from which to watch the 'zoo' below. / Website: www.the-collection.co.uk Details: 5pm-midnight. Food: till 11.30pm. DJ: nightly. Live music: mixed genres.

Le Coq D'Argent EC2

1 Poultry 7395 5000 9–2C

*On a hot summer's day in the City, there's no better way
to relax than by sipping something refreshing at this impressive
sixth-floor complex, which overlooks the Bank of England. It has
an amazing rooftop terrace, plus 'garden' tables. Inside,
the drinking area segues into the large, anonymous and pricey
dining room – yes, you're in D&D (fka Conran) territory.*
/ **Website:** www.danddlondon.com **Details:** Mon-Fri 11.30am-11pm,
Sat 6.30pm-11pm, Sun noon-3pm. **Food:** L till 3pm, bar snacks till 10pm.

Cork & Bottle WC2

44-46 Cranbourn St 7734 7807 4–3B

*Nestling besides a sex-shop, this cramped Leicester Square
basement has been a reliable West End retreat for four
decades, and still makes an ideal pre-theatre rendezvous.
It certainly isn't cheap, but the outstanding wine list reflects the
enthusiasm of connoisseur-patron Don Hewitson. Solid old-style
wine bar fare is available.* / **Website:** www.corkandbottle.net
Details: Mon-Sat 9am-11.30, Sun noon-10.30pm. **Food:** till 11.30pm, Sun till
10.30pm.

Cottons NW1

55 Chalk Farm Rd 7485 8388 8–2B

*They're serious about their 'rhums' – a range of over 250 –
and their cocktails at London's leading Caribbean-themed joint,
where drinkers congregate in the 'Jamaica Bar' at the front.
Press on and have a full meal in one of the dining rooms
('Margarita', 'St Lucia', or 'Barbados'), and results are up-and-
down, but a very jolly vibe is a constant throughout.*
/ **Website:** www.cottons-restaurant.co.uk **Details:** Mon-Thu 5pm-11.30pm,
Fri 5pm-1am, Sat 1pm-1am, Sun 1pm-11pm. **Food:** Mon-Thu 6pm-10.30pm,
Fri 6pm-11.30pm, Sat 1pm-4pm & 6pm-11.30pm, Sun 1pm-10.30pm. **DJ:** Fri
& Sat. **Happy hour:** 5pm-7pm.

The Couch W1

97-99 Dean St 7287 0150 3–1D

*Run by an outfit called Thomas & Carter, this big corner-site –
with its rustic old tables, brown-and-cream décor and gilt
mirrors – is at the more refined end of the corporate boozer
market. It makes a useful Soho stand-by, but beware popularity
with the local post-office crowd.*
/ **Website:** www.innventiveoperations.com **Food:** till 10pm. **DJ:** Sat night.

The Cow W2

89 Westbourne Park Rd   7221 0021   6–1B

*Physically in Bayswater but spiritually in Notting Hill,
Tom Conran's wonderfully atmospheric pub remains one of the
key watering holes in the area. The packed public bar manages
a pretty good approximation to rural Ireland (if you ignore the
crowds of trustafarians, that is), and the seafood dishes –
oysters a house speciality – and Guinness are very good.
Upstairs, there's a quieter little dining room.*
*/ **Website:** www.thecowlondon.co.uk **Details:** Mon-Sat noon-11pm,
Sun noon-10.30pm; no Amex. **Food:** L till 4pm, D till 10.30pm.*

Crazy Bear W1

26-28 Whitfield St   7631 0088   2–1C

*Few places in town have had as much money thrown at their
design as this stunning cocktail bar, in sumptuous cellars
beneath a glamorous oriental Thai restaurant (hidden-away
near Goodge Street tube). It's full of plushly furnished nooks
with sprawly leather banquettes (and loos where the designers
went bonkers with crystal and mirrors). The only downside
is that when it's busy (often), the noise level can be very high.*
*/ **Website:** www.crazybeargroup.co.uk **Details:** Mon-Fri noon-midnight,
Sat 6pm-midnight, closed Sun. **Food:** till 11pm.*

The Cricketers TW9

Maids Of Honour Rw, The Grn   8940 4372   1–4A

*Not many pubs in London suburbs still overlook charming, leafy
cricket pitches. This 19th-century Greene King hostelry,
overlooking Richmond Green, is one of the few with such
a picturebook location. It's cosy and characterful enough inside,
but it's in summer – when you can take your pint on to the
grass (or into the courtyard) – that it really comes into its own.*
*/ **Details:** Mon-Sat noon-11pm, Sun noon-10.30pm. **Food:** till 10pm,
weekends till 7pm.*

Crooked Billet SW19

14-15 Crooked Billet   8946 4942   10–2B

*In summer, the crowds from this recently refurbished Young's
hostelry and its neighbouring twin (the Hand in Hand) seem
to take over the green after which the pub is named
(or perhaps it's vice-versa?). It does have other attractions
however – the interior is very characterful and cosy, and there
is a good variety of pub grub (and of wines by the glass). They
celebrate all things German here, so beer aficionados should
visit during 'Oktoberfest'.*
*/ **Website:** www.thecrookedbilletwimbledon.co.uk **Details:** Sun-Thu
11am-11pm, Fri & Sat 11am-midnight. **Food:** L till 3pm, D till 10pm, Sun till
8pm.*

Cross Keys WC2

31 Endell St   7836 5185   4–2D
If you think the facade if this foliage-covered Covent Garden-fringe pub is ornate, wait till you get inside. The modestly-scaled interior houses a cornucopia of ornaments, mirrors, pictures, horse brasses, road signs, brass pots, and even the odd stuffed fish. As if that weren't enough, there's a small collection of Beatles memorabilia, and a napkin signed by Elvis Presley.
*/ **Food:** till 2.30pm.*

Cross Keys SW3

1 Lawrence St   7349 9111   5–3C
It's something of a surprise, deep in the backstreets of Old Chelsea, to come across a boozer which was substantially jazzed up (and had an impressive dining-conservatory added) a few years ago. It has a really buzzy atmosphere, though, and is a very popular destination with younger locals.
*/ **Website:** www.thexkeys.co.uk **Food:** till 10pm.*

The Crown NW2

301 Cricklewood Broadway   8452 4175   1–1B
*They don't build 'em like this any more. This absolutely ginormous Victorian tavern (rebuilt in 1889) is a dominating presence in the heart of Cricklewood. Nowadays it's annexed to an hotel, and comprises five bars (four of which are in the original building). With its stained glass, open fires, and leather sofas, it's just the venue for a cosy evening's imbibing, in a not-overprovided part of town. / **Website:** www.thecrowncricklewood.co.uk*

Crown & Goose NW1

100 Arlington Rd   7485 8008   8–3B
*This agreeable side street gastropub of long standing is particularly worth seeking out if you're wanting to escape the mayhem of Camden Town's main drag, and it makes an ideal place for a drink and a chinwag. Bitters include London Pride and John Smith, and the usual range of lagers is also on offer. (There are perennial rumours that the site is to be redeveloped, so check it's still there if you're thinking of making a special journey.) / **Website:** www.crownandgoose.com **Details:** Mon noon–11pm, Tue-Thu & Sun noon-midnight , Fri & Sat noon-2am; no Amex. **Food:** till 10pm, Sun till 9pm.*

The Crown & Greyhound SE21

73 Dulwich Village   8299 4976   1–4D

This vast, listed Victorian pub (Mitchells and Butler) is situated in the heart of leafy Dulwich Village and caters to a crowd of all ages. With its original fittings, huge rear beer-garden and not-bad food, it's no surprise that it's treasured locally (and not just because pubs are thin on the ground hereabouts). Charles Dickens wrote here. / Website: www.thecrownandgreyhound.co.uk **Food:** *till 10pm.*

The Crown Tavern EC1

43 Clerkenwell Gn   7253 4973   9–1A

This atmospheric Victorian pub on a corner overlooking Clerkenwell Green – originally a music hall, in which Karl Marx once spoke – has been made over in recent times in a simple modern style, with muted colours and low-key lighting. It's a comfortable place whose large range of tipples includes no fewer than 68 bottled beers. / Details: noon-midnight. **Food:** *till 10pm.*

Cuba Libre N1

72 Upper St   7354 9998   8–3D

A large Cuban bar-restaurant in Islington, whose muraled, atmospheric decor and energetic style has kept it busy for almost two decades now. The South American food may help make the place an all-round party destination, but is not an attraction in its own right. / Website: www.cubalibrelondon.co.uk **Details:** *Mon-Thu 11am-midnight, Fri & Sat 11am-2am, Sun noon-9.30pm; no Amex.* **Food:** *Mon-Thu till 10pm, Fri-Sat till 11pm, Sun till 9.30pm.* **Happy hour:** *Mon-Fri 5pm-8pm, Sat & Sun noon-8pm.* **Cover charge** *may apply.*

The Cutty Sark Tavern SE10

4-6 Ballast Quay   8858 3146   1–3D

A great get-away-from-the-crowds destination for a weekend trip to Greenwich, this attractive 17th-century freehouse benefits from not actually being located anywhere particularly near its namesake vessel. Seating outside, right by the river. / Details: no Amex. **Food:** *till 9pm, Sat till 10pm.*

The Dacre Arms SE13

11 Kingwood Pl   8852 6779   1–4D

It's a bit out on a limb, but this privately owned pub is worth knowing about if you're looking for a drink down Lee/Blackheath way. With its half-panelled booths and the cosy clutter strewn around, this is your classic traditional boozer, with a beer garden at the rear. / Details: no credit cards.

De Hems W1

11 Macclesfield St   7437 2494   4–3A

The only Dutch bar in London is a cavernous pub, well-known by virtue of its ornate exterior and prominent location (on the northern fringe of Chinatown). Those who hate crowded pubs will loathe it – for serious drinkers of Dutch (and Belgian) ales, though, this is the place. / **Website:** www.dehems.co.uk
Details: Mon-Sat noon-midnight, Sun noon-10.30pm. **Food:** till 10pm.

Detroit WC2

35 Earlham St   7240 2662   4–2C

One of London's earliest design-led bars, this north-Covent Garden venture – whose 'Star Wars meets the Flintstones' décor has little obviously to do with Motown – has stood the test of time surprisingly well. An intimate place, with lots of nooks and crannies, it puts quite an emphasis on cocktails. / **Website:** www.detroit-bar.com **Details:** Mon-Sat 5pm-midnight, closed Sun. **Food:** bar food till 10.30pm. **DJ:** Fri & Sat. **Happy hour:** 5pm-7pm. **Cover charge may apply.**

Devonshire Terrace EC2

Devonshire Sq   7256 3233   9–2D

A large newcomer on the City drinking scene, this hard-edged bar/restaurant, near Liverpool Street, offers many semi-al fresco tables, in the atrium of the Devonshire Square office development. Some have surprisingly impressive views. / **Website:** www.devonshireterrace.co.uk **Details:** Mon-Fri 8am-midnight, closed Sat & Sun. **Food:** noon-11pm.

Dial
Mountbatten Hotel WC2

20 Monmouth St   7836 4300   4–2B

The large windows of this hotel bar (and restaurant) overlooking Covent Garden's Seven Dials mini-roundabout help make it a great people-watching venue. Mock-croc pouffes, leather chairs and dark wood surrounds create quite a chic setting, if in a fairly conservative style (ideal, say, for a business drink). / **Website:** www.radissonedwardian.com **Details:** Mon-Wed 5.30pm-10.30pm, Thu-Sat 5.30pm-11pm, closed Sun. **Food:** Mon-Wed till 10.30pm, Thu-Sat till 11pm.

The Dickens Inn E1

St Katharine's Way   7488 2208   9–3D

For an 'away-from-it-all' waterside location that's just a few minutes walk from the City, this mega-scale establishment, near Tower Bridge, has got an awful lot to recommend it. As the name suggests, however, you're talking serious touristville, but the terraces, with views over the marina, are surprisingly pleasant. / **Website:** *www.dickensinn.co.uk* **Food:** *till 10pm.*

The Dog & Duck W1

18 Bateman St   7494 0697   4–2A

This timeless Nicholson's corner pub is the epitome of a cosy Soho institution. Sat upstairs with a pint in the 'George Orwell Bar & Dining Room', you may be tempted to reflect that not much has changed since the great man supped here back in the '40s... except, perhaps, the dress sense of the younger patrons. / **Details:** *Mon-Thu 11am-11pm, Fri & Sat 11am-11.30pm, Sun noon-10.30pm.* **Food:** *till 10pm.*

Dogstar SW9

389 Coldharbour Ln   7733 7515   10–2D

One of the first bar-clubs to open in London in the mid-90s, the Dogstar became a byword for hip and happening in cutting-edge Brixton. Loud and serving until late on Fri and Sat evenings, it's also the place for a good Sun lunch (with '80s disco afterwards, to aid recovery from the night before). / **Website:** *www.antic-ltd.com/dogstar* **Details:** *Mon-Thu 4pm-2am, Fri 4pm-4am, Sat noon-4am & Sun noon-2am; no Amex.* **DJ:** *nightly.* **Live music:** *Thu.* **Cover charge may apply.**

$ EC1

2 Exmouth Mkt   7278 0077   9–1A

The most obvious feature of this good-looking Farringdon pub-conversion – which has a "Grills & Martinis" theme – is its ground-floor brasserie, which has a very buzzy atmosphere. For those just in search of a drink, however, it is the hidden-gem basement bar – notable for its cosiness – which is particularly worth seeking out. / **Website:** *www.dollargrills.com* **Details:** *noon-1am.* **Food:** *Mon-Sun, Sun brunch.*

Donovan Bar
Brown's Hotel W1

30 Albemarle St   7493 6020   3–2C

*This swish, relaxing bar – adorned with photographs by noted snapper Terence Donovan – is perhaps the most successful part of Rocco Forte's revamp of this ultra-traditional townhouse hotel, just off Piccadilly. It offers a good range of wines, and a better choice of cocktails. / **Website:** www.brownshotel.com*
Details: *Mon-Sat 11am-1am, Sun noon-midnight . **Food:** always available.*

Dorchester Bar
Dorchester Hotel W1

53 Park Ln   7629 8888   3–3A

Decorated in bizarre (Dante's-Inferno-meets-motorway café) style, the bar of this famous Mayfair hotel totally lacks the chic ambience one might expect. There is another, much nicer, bar at the end of the hotel's central promenade, but the best bar at this address is China Tang (see also).
*/ **Website:** www.dorchesterhotel.com* **Details:** *Mon-Thu noon-1am, Fri & Sat noon-2am, Sun noon-midnight . **Food:** till 11.45pm, Sun till 10.30pm. **DJ:** Mon & Fri.*

Dove E8

24-28 Broadway Mkt   7275 7617   1–2D

*An eccentric 'freehouse & kitchen', in artsy Broadway Market. It has a cosy feel to it, and serves a selection of 100 or so Belgian beers and six draught bitters to a loyal fan club. Basic pub fare is also available. / **Website:** www.belgianbars.com*
Details: *Sun-Thu noon-11pm, Fri-Sat noon-midnight; no Amex. **Food:** till 10pm.*

Dove W6

19 Upper Mall   8748 9474   7–2B

*It has a great location, but that's not the only selling-point of this Dickensian Fullers tavern – the classiest of the many traditional pubs by the river at Hammersmith. It's a particular favourite for Sun lunch, and it is as difficult in summer to get a seat on the small, riverside terrace as it is in winter to nab a spot by the fire. No children. / **Food:** L till 3pm, D till 9pm no food, Sun till 4pm.*

Dover Castle W1

43 Weymouth Mews   7580 4412   3–1B

*This Sam Smith's boozer, in a cobbled mews near Portland
Place, offers more than usual in the way of character. If you're
looking for a place for drink (and, maybe, a spot of pub grub)
that's close to the West End but without crowds or Muzak,
this may well be it.* / **Details:** *Mon-Sat noon-11pm, closed Sun.* **Food:** *L
till 2pm, D till 8.30pm.*

The Dovetail EC1

9-10 Jerusalem Pas   7490 7321   9–1A

*The best of London's (admittedly small) crop of Belgian beer
halls, this hidden-away Clerkenwell spot offers 101 different
brews. Draught options range from the mainstream to the
obscure, and the sheer variety of bottled beers (Trappist,
Lambic, Geueze, white, fruit and pilsners, to name but a few
types) is mind-boggling. Eccentric décor (think kitsch Gothic
monastery) and the food are further attractions.*
/ **Website:** *www.dovepubs.com* **Details:** *Mon-Sat noon-11pm, Sun 1pm-9pm;
no Amex.* **Food:** *L till 3pm, D till 10pm, Sat noon-10pm, Sun 1pm-9pm.*

Dragon Bar E1

138-139 Shoreditch High St   311 8255   9–1D

*In early-2009, the long-standing 'Sosho' speakeasy upped sticks
to this new home nearby. The ownership may be the same,
but the old and new locations couldn't be more different –
the beatnik easy-to-miss former establishment has been
replaced by a swish sort of place (with red velvet, low lights,
and candles), prominently-situated on the Shoreditch strip.*
/ **Details:** *Sun-Tue noon-midnight, Wed noon-1am, Thu-Sat noon-2am;
no Amex.* **DJ:** *Thu-Sat.*

Dreambagsjaguarshoes E2

34-36 Kingsland Rd   7729 5830   9–1D

*The epitome of Shoreditch style – or a parody, if you prefer –
this is the bar that hides behind two unreconstructed shop
fronts, and completely changes its look every six weeks or so,
when a new artist or illustrator is put in charge. Now settled
into comfortable middle age (by local standards), it can seem
a bit less self-consciously hip than was once the case. Well,
all things are relative...* / **Website:** *www.dreambagsjaguarshoes.com*
Details: *Mon 5pm-midnight, Tue-Fri noon-1am, Sat 5pm-1am,
Sun noon-12.30am; no Amex.* **Food:** *till 11am .*

The Duke of Cambridge N1

30 St Peters St   7359 3066   1–2C

This Islington backstreet boozer was ten years ago the first — and still today one of the few — certified as 'Organic' by the Soil Association. And that goes for the wine and beers (from the Freedom and Pitfield breweries) too! Whether that's actually what keeps it packed out with trendy locals is a moot point — could it just be that they like the cosy and comfy vibe of its shabby-chic interior? / Website: www.dukeorganic.co.uk
Details: Mon-Sat noon-11pm, Sun noon-10.30pm; no Amex. **Food:** Mon-Fri L till 3pm, D till 10.30pm, Sat L till 3.30pm D till 10.30pm, Sun L till 3.30pm D till 10pm.

Duke on the Green SW6

235 New King's Rd   7736 2777   10–1B

Overlooking Parson's Green, this stylish renovation of a very large Young's boozer has quickly created a big local following, thanks to its pleasant atmosphere, and good food. Rugby on the big screens too. / Website: www.dukeonthegreen.co.uk
Details: Mon-Fri 11am-midnight, Sat 10.30am-midnight, Sun 10.30am-11.30am. **Food:** till 10.30pm, Sun till 9.30pm.

The Duke's Head SW15

8 Lower Richmond Rd   8788 2552   10–1A

A huge bay window overlooking the Thames is one of the prime features of this impressive Victorian Young's pub. One of the most spacious and civilised traditional boozers in town, it received a 'gastro' make-over a couple of years ago, and serves very decent food nowadays. When the weather's fine you can take your drink outside. Naturally, this is key Boat Race boozer, as it's right by the start.
/ Website: www.dukesheadputney.co.uk **Details:** Mon-Wed 11am-11pm, Thu 11am-midnight, Sun noon-11pm, Fri & Sat 11am-1am. **Food:** till 9.30pm, Fri & Sat till 10pm.

Dukes Hotel Bar SW1

35 St James's Pl   7491 4840   3–4C

This smart and discreet St James's establishment, recently refurbished in essentially traditional style, is one of the few central hotels which still exudes a rather 'proper' charm. It has a particular reputation for its martinis.
/ Website: www.dukeshotel.com **Details:** noon-10.30pm . **Food:** till 4.30pm.

Dulwich Wood House SE26

39 Sydenham Hill   8693 5666   1–4D

*Recently subject to a major refurbishment, this large and airy hostelry is part of the Young's estate, and therefore worth knowing about in an area, near Forest Hill, without a huge number of obvious competing attractions. The building, originally a house, was designed by Sir Joseph Paxton, architect of Crystal Palace. There are several bars, as well as a big garden. / **Website:** www.dulwichwoodhouse.com **Food:** L noon-3pm, D 6-10pm.*

The George Bar
Durrants Hotel W1

26-32 George St   7935 8131   3–1A

*This quintessential English hotel first opened in 1790, and it has been in its current ownership for nearly 90 years. With its mahogany panelling, the décor is as traditional as you could possibly want, and the calming bar offers welcome relief after a hard day's graft (or shopping in fashionable Marylebone High Street, nearby). / **Website:** www.durrantshotel.co.uk **Details:** Mon-Fri 11am-11pm, Sat & Sun 11am-10.30pm. **Food:** L till 2.45pm, D till 10.15pm.*

E&O W11

14 Blenheim Cr   7229 5454   6–1A

*Will Ricker's modernistic 'Eastern and Oriental' bar and restaurant is a firmly-established linchpin of the Notting Hill set (if not, perhaps, the star-spotter's paradise it once was). The restaurant is an attraction in itself, but the bar is no second best, offering a fantastic buzz as well as a good range of cocktails. / **Website:** www.rickerrestaurants.com **Details:** noon-midnight. **Food:** till 11pm.*

The Eagle EC1

159 Farringdon Rd   7837 1353   9–1A

*The pub that broke the mould – this stripped-down Clerkenwell boozer (revamped in 1991) was the first to be recognised as a 'gastropub', with its combination of quality Mediterranean cuisine and wines, and yet still offering the prospect of a nice pint. Legions of rivals have come and gone, but the consistent scrum of would-be diners here confirms that the place has managed, more or less, to keep up with the pack. / **Details:** Mon-Sat noon-11pm, Sun noon-5pm; no Amex. **Food:** Mon-Fri L till 3pm, D 6.30pm-10.30pm, Sat L 12.30pm-3.30pm, D 6.30pm-10pm.*

Eagle Bar Diner W1

4-5 Rathbone Pl   7637 1418   4–1A

*A burger-diner just north of Oxford Street somehow doesn't
sound the trendiest of destinations, but cynics may
be confounded by a visit to this cool joint. The scoff is good –
and so are the shakes – but it's the cocktails and the vibe which
draw the evening crowds.* / **Website:** www.eaglebardiner.com
Details: Mon-Wed noon-11pm, Thu & Fri noon-1am, Sat 10am-1am,
Sun 11am-6pm; no Amex. **Food:** Mon-Wed till 10.45pm, Thu-Sat till 11.45,
Sun till 6. **DJ:** Wed 7pm, Thu-Sat 7.30pm.

The Earl Spencer SW18

260-262 Merton Rd   8870 9244   10–2B

*This large, popular gastroboozer remains a key Southfields
destination, perhaps because they really do take care about the
food, and offer a menu that changes daily. A lively place, if with
a rather barn-like setting, it extends a warm welcome to all its
customers (including children).* / **Website:** www.theearlspencer.co.uk
Details: Mon-Thu noon-11pm, Fri & Sat noon-midnight, Sun noon-10.30pm.
Food: Mon-Sat L 12.30pm-2.30pm, D 7pm-10pm, Sun L noon-3pm,
D 7pm-9.30pm.

Easton WC1

22 Easton St   7278 7608   9–1A

*It's not actually in Exmouth Market, but this popular
gastroboozer is easily visible from Clerkenwell's trendiest street,
a minute or so's walk away. That very much sets the tone
of the place – a bit grungy, but offering a classic pub setting for
some quite interesting cooking, as well as a good range of beers
and wines.* / **Details:** Mon-Fri noon-11pm, Fri & Sat 5.30pm-1am,
Sun 12.30pm-10.30pm; no Amex. **Food:** L till 3pm, D till 10pm, Sun L till
4pm, D till 9.30pm.

Ebury SW1

11 Pimlico Rd   7730 6784   5–2D

*Neither Pimlico, where this large establishment is situated,
nor neighbouring Belgravia has that many groovy places to eat
and drink. In part, we can't help thinking it's this lack of local
competition which makes this big bar-cum-brasserie-cum-
restaurant quite as popular as it is, but it's undoubtedly a key
destination in these parts.* / **Website:** www.thebury.co.uk
Details: noon-11pm. **Food:** noon-3.30pm, 6pm-10.30pm.

Eclipse

111-113 Walton St SW3   7581 0123   5–2C
158 Old Brompton Rd SW5   7259 2577   5–2B
57 High St SW19   8944 7722   10–2B

*This trio of elegant SW London cocktail bars (part of the group who own 'Boujis', and billing themselves as "the home of the irresistible watermelon martini") doesn't aim for fireworks, but for convivial, comfy glamour. They've lost a couple of branches in recent times, but those that survive still seem very popular. / **Website:** www.eclipse-ventures.com.*

The Edgar Wallace WC2

40 Essex St   7353 3120   2–2D
*Edgar Wallace was a prolific thriller-writer who lived in this part of town at the beginning of the last century. This attractive pub was named after him on the centenary of his birth in 1975, and displays memorabilia from his life. Barristers from the neighbouring Temple makes up much of the clientele, but the place is also well on the tourist beat.
/ **Website:** www.edgarwallacepub.com **Details:** closed Sat & Sun; no Amex.
Food: till 9.30pm.*

The Edge W1

11 Soho Sq   7439 1313   4–1A
*Spilling into the square on sunny afternoons, and heaving at weekends, this is one of the longest-running Soho success-stories, catering mainly to a gay crowd. Three floors offer a range of music styles. Start an evening here and you could easily find yourself staying all night... not least because the crush can make it difficult to move around.
/ **Website:** www.edgesoho.co.uk **Details:** Mon-Sat noon-1am,
Sun 4pm-11.30pm; no Amex. **Food:** Tue-Sun till 9. **DJ:** Tue, Fri & Sat
(sometimes Thu). **Live music:** Wed.*

Eight Bells SW6

89 Fulham High St   7736 6307   10–1B
*This small Georgian tavern, near Putney Bridge tube, claims to be the oldest in Fulham, having occupied this site since the late-17th century. It's a characterful, tightly-packed panelled place, with a U-shaped bar – very much a civilised local.
/ **Food:** L till 3pm, D till 9pm.*

Eight Over Eight SW3

392 King's Rd   7349 9934   5–3B

*Having helped establish the trendy East End (Cicada, Great Eastern) and having conquered Notting Hill, Will Ricker brought his brand of oriental tapas restaurant-plus-cool-lounge-bar to Chelsea a few years ago. Like its siblings, this sleekly laid-out venue has become a local style magnet, and also does great cocktails and very decent food. / **Website:** www.rickerrestaurants.com* **Details:** *Mon-Sat noon-midnight, Sun 6pm-11pm .* **Food:** *till midnight.*

1802 E14

1 India Quay, Warehouse, Hertsmere Rd
7358 2702   11–1C

*Across a footbridge from Canary Wharf, this airy warehouse-conversion is one of the nicer places for a drink in the environs of the east-London money-factories. Run by upmarket caterers/restaurateurs Searcy's, it's less themed than some of its near neighbours. Like them, however, it benefits from very extensive outside seating, and an impressive view. / **Website:** www.1802docklands.co.uk* **Details:** *Mon-Fri 11am-11pm, Sat noon-6pm, Sun noon-8.30pm (5.30pm in winter).* **Food:** *Mon-Sat 5pm-11pm.* **DJ:** *Thu & Fri.* **Happy hour:** *Mon-Fri 6pm-8pm.*

El Vino's

47 Fleet St EC4   7353 6786   9–2A
Alban Gate, 125 London Wall EC2   7600 6377   9–2B
30 New Bridge St EC4   7236 4534   9–3A

*Old-fashioned, but in an attractive and welcoming way, these famous City wine bars remain extremely popular with pinstripes of all ages. The Martin Lane branch (which trades under the name Olde Wine Shades, see also) is the oldest wine house in the Square Mile. All branches offer simple but satisfying cooking (with the option of restaurant service). / **Website:** www.elvino.co.uk.*

The Elbow Room

103 Westbourne Grove W2   7221 5211   6–1B
89-91 Chapel Mkt N1   7278 3244   8–3D
97-113 Curtain Rd EC2   7613 1316   9–1D

*Flock wallpapered walls, neon lights and purple-felted tables have helped turn these pool hall bars into funky places to hang out. The original (W2) branch is the calmest – all the other venues are DJ bars. Sink a few beers and American-style snacks (burgers, nachos, etc) while waiting for a table to be vacated. (At peak times there are long queues, and you're limited to an hour's play.) / **Website:** www.elbow-room.co.uk.*

The Electric Birdcage SW1

11 Haymarket   7839 2424   4–4A

In the heart of touristy Theatreland, it's a surprise to find this comfortable cocktail bar, lavishly decorated in whimsical style. During the daytime – when they offer some very decent dim sum, and so on – it makes a very handy place for a light meal too. / **Website:** www.electricbirdcage.com **Details:** Mon-Wed noon–11pm, Thu & Fri noon-4am, Sat 5pm-4am. **Food:** always available. **DJ:** nightly. **Cover charge may apply.**

Electricity Showrooms N1

39a Hoxton Sq   7739 3939   9–1D

When it opened in the '90s, this prominently situated landmark sported an ultra-utilitarian, white-walled look. There's no evidence of that nowadays, however, as it's been glammed up over the years, now sporting a style that's almost Edwardian in some places. The ground-floor bar gives little hint as to the major dance floor in the basement (which lights up Saturday Night Fever-style). / **Website:** www.electricityshowrooms.co.uk **Details:** Mon-Thu noon-midnight, Fri & Sat noon-1am. **Food:** till 10.30pm. **DJ:** most nights.

Elephant & Castle W8

40 Holland St   7937 6382   5–1A

A cute location, in a backwater just off Kensington High Street, adds to the appeal of this cosy and traditional Georgian boozer. When it's busy (often), it can be a bit of a squeeze, at which times many punters prefer to drink in the street outside (or, if very lucky, at a table on the tiny terrace). / **Details:** no Amex. **Food:** till 9pm, Sun till 4pm .

Elephant Royale E14

Westferry Rd   7987 7999   11–2C

Although the dining operation dominates at this Thai restaurant at the tip of the Isle of Dogs, there is also quite a big bar scene. The interior design is a bit tacky (well actually it's very tacky), but on a summer's day you can drink on the nice riverside terrace, which has a magnificent view of Greenwich over the water. Arrive early for an evening table. No children, except for Sun buffet. / **Website:** www.elephantroyale.com **Details:** Mon-Thu noon-3pm & 5.30pm-11.30pm, Fri & Sat noon-midnight, Sun noon-11pm. **Food:** till 1 hour before closing.

Elk Bar SW6

587 Fulham Rd   7385 6940   5–4A

There's something for everyone at this lively, large, dark red
Fulham bar – a Mint Group production – which comes
complete with a beer garden. By the prevailing standards
of SW6 this is quite a cool place, but they're also quite happy
to play cheesy music when it suits them. / **Website:** www.elkbar.com
Details: Mon-Wed noon-11pm, Thu-Sun noon-midnight. **Food:** till 9pm.
Happy hour: 5pm-7pm.

The Elk in the Woods N1

39 Camden Pas   7226 3535   8–3D

In the cute lane behind the Islington Antiques Market,
this intimate, contemporary-style spot is a cut well-above
most other watering holes hereabouts. If you're looking for
a decent cocktail or glass of wine – plus, perhaps, some high
quality, if fairly simple nosh – this may well be just the place for
you. / **Website:** www.the-elk-in-the-woods.co.uk **Details:** 10.30am-10.30pm;
no Amex. **Food:** Wed-Mon all day, Tue noon-10.30pm.

Ember EC1

99-100 Turnmill St   7490 3985   9–1A

A "cutting edge style bar" (well, that's what the management
says) – this popular operation by Farringdon tube certainly has
a handy location and a certain quirky charm to recommend it.
/ **Details:** Mon-Tue 11am-midnight, Wed & Thu 11am-1am, Fri & Sat
11am-2.30am, Sun 10am-10.30pm. **Food:** Mon-Fri noon-10pm, Sat & Sun
10am-10pm.

The Endurance W1

90 Berwick St   7437 2944   3–2D

Berwick Street, with its fruit market, is amongst the
most characterful of Soho's seedier thoroughfares. This old
boozer (once called the King of Corsica), in the middle of the
street, was scrubbed up a few years ago, and now attracts
younger bloods in search of a retro pub experience. And not
a bad one at that. / **Website:** www.theendurance.co.uk **Details:** Mon-Sat
noon-11pm, Sun noon-4pm. **Food:** till 4pm.

The Engineer NW1

65 Gloucester Ave   7722 0950   8–3B

*This legendary Primrose Hill establishment can claim to have helped found the gastropub revolution, and – with its cool bar, atmospheric restaurant and dependable cooking – continues to draw a glamorous and trendy crowd from far and wide. Get there early if you want a seat, especially in the great garden in summer. / **Website:** www.the-engineer.com **Details:** Mon-Sat 9am-11pm, Sun 9am-10.30pm; no Amex. **Food:** weekdays noon-3pm, 7pm-10.30pm, weekends 12.30pm-4pm, 7pm-10pm.*

The Enterprise SW3

35 Walton St   7584 3148   5–2C

*A 'feel-good' ambience has helped make this comfortable pub-conversion near Harrods – half bar/half bistro – a long-running success-story, popular with a well-heeled local crowd. The food's no big deal, but you may well still have to wait for a table – you can always sink a bottle of bubbly while you wait. / **Website:** www.christophersgrill.com **Details:** noon-11pm. **Food:** L till 3pm, D till 10.15pm.*

The Establishment SW6

45-47 Parson's Green Ln   7384 2418   10–1B

*Bold geometric wallpaper underpins the '70s-retro styling of this well-acclaimed new bar/restaurant opposite Parson's Green tube. Not everyone is impressed by the food, but, as a place to chill out over a few drinks, it has a lot going for it. / **Website:** www.theestablishment.com **Details:** Mon-Sat noon-midnight, Sun noon-10.30pm. **Food:** till 10.30pm.*

Exhibit SW12

12 Balham Station Rd   8772 6556   10–2C

*Fish tanks in the wall and seriously low-slung sofas complete the modernistic, Scandinavian-style décor of this cool Balham bar. Its name is appropriate, as this is definitely a place for posing, and the outside tables – with fine views of Sainsbury's car park – are very popular in summer. You can eat in the bar, and there's also a restaurant upstairs. / **Website:** www.theexhibit.co.uk **Details:** Mon-Thu 5pm-midnight, Fri 4pm-2am, Sat 11.30am-2am, Sun 11am-11pm; no Amex. **Food:** till 11pm. **Happy hour:** 5pm-8pm.*

Favela Chic EC2

91-93 Great Eastern St   7613 5228   9–1D

This eclectic joint in Shoreditch is a spin-off from a Parisian outfit. Amidst a jungle of reclaimed wood, flock wallpaper and greenery, its serves up an extensive and pricey cocktail menu, plus Latino food and music. Music is a mix of Brazilian and French hip hop, with some reggae and drum 'n' bass mixed in (and maybe even a bit of rock 'n' roll).
/ **Website:** www.favelachic.com **Details:** Tue-Fri 5.30pm-1am, Sat 5.30pm-2am, closed Sun & Mon. **Food:** Tue-Fri 5.30pm-1am, Sat 5.30pm-2am. **DJ:** Fri & Sat.

The Fellow N1

24 York Way   7833 4395   8–3C

How times change. If you haven't been up King's Cross way for a bit, the area is (finally!) starting to look up, and this new venture is part of the ever-smarter strip leading up to the swanky new King's Place development. Downstairs is a modern pub with open kitchen, while on the first floor there's a more loungy bar, complete with heated roof terrace.
/ **Website:** www.thefellow.co.uk **Details:** noon-late, cocktail bar 5pm-late. **Food:** till 10pm. **DJ:** Fri & Sat.

5th View
Waterstones W1

203-206 Piccadilly   7851 2433   3–3D

When we first heard about it, we thought the fifth floor bar at Waterstone's flagship store (which has interesting rooftop views) might be a locals' secret – a stylish destination for a quiet drink above the tourist hell of Piccadilly. Unfortunately, the secret's out (it can get crowded) but it's certainly a handy spot. / **Website:** www.5thview.co.uk **Details:** Mon-Sat 10am-10pm, Sun noon-5pm. **Food:** Mon-Fri, Sun noon-3pm Sat till 4pm.

Filthy MacNasty's EC1

68 Amwell St   7837 6067   9–1A

A large and sinister sign advertises the presence of this scruffy-looking 'Whiskey Café', in the oddly characterful no-man's-land between Clerkenwell and Islington. There's quite an emphasis on Guinness and whiskeys, but this likeable (and, to fans, legendary) joint is by no means your standard Irish theme bar, and its range of attractions includes literary readings and live music. Thai food too, plus a traditional Sun lunch.
/ **Website:** www.filthymacnastys.com **Details:** Mon-Sat noon-11pm, Sun noon-10.30pm; no Amex. **Food:** L till 3pm (except Sat & Sun), D till 9.30pm (except Sun).

The Fire Stables SW19

27-29 Church Rd   8946 3197   10–2B

When this large, strikingly-designed bar/restaurant was opened a few years ago, it was just the kind of trendy destination sleepy old Wimbledon Village desperately needed. It still has few rivals hereabouts and gets pretty packed with a crowd who come as much to eat as to drink – both in the rear restaurant and also at the bare wooden tables at the front.
/ **Website:** www.firestableswimbledon.co.uk **Food:** Mon-Fri L till 4pm & D till 10.30pm, Sat L till 4pm & D till 10.30pm, Sun L till 4pm & D till 10pm.

5B Urban Bar E14

27 Three Colt St   7537 1601   11–1B

This Docklands boozer has been given a trademark 'make-over' by the Urban Bar company – its exterior is zebra-striped, its interior neo-Gothic, and it sports Oz and Kiwi flags in the window. Fancy dress nights twice a week. You have been warned. / **Details:** Mon-Fri 5pm-1am, Sat & Sun 5pm-2am. **Food:** till midnight. **DJ:** Fri. **Live music:** Tue.

The Flask NW3

14 Flask Walk   7435 4580   8–1A

Not to be confused with the possibly even more famous Highgate Flask, this serious beer-drinkers' Victorian pub, bristling with CAMRA awards, is conveniently located on a quiet, pedestrianised lane in the centre of Hampstead. The front bars – divided by a charming, original screen – are more characterful than the rear conservatory.
/ **Website:** www.theflaskhampstead.co.uk **Details:** Mon-Thu 11am-11pm, Fri & Sat 11am-midnight, Sun noon-10.30pm; no Amex. **Food:** Mon-Sat noon-10pm, Sun noon-9pm.

The Flask N6

77 Highgate West Hill   8348 7346   8–1B

Idyllically located in the prettiest part of Highgate, this large coaching inn is early-18th century in origin, and feels almost as if it were deep in the country. Its big yard gets full to overflowing on sunny days. In early 2009, Mitchells & Butler sold it to Fuller's, but sweeping changes seem unlikely.
/ **Details:** no Amex. **Food:** L till 3pm, D till 10pm.

Florence SE24

131-133 Dulwich Rd   7326 4987   1–4D

Opposite Brockwell Park, this old corner pub has recently emerged with a shiny, bright new look. It's now also a micro-brewery, with a range of vats at the side of the room, producing the likes of their very own Weasel bitter. Other features include a pleasant conservatory and large outside area.
/ **Website:** www.capitalpubcompany.com/florence **Details:** Mon-Thu 11am-midnight, Fri 11am-1.30am, Sat 10am-1.30am, Sun 10am-midnight; no Amex. **Food:** Mon-Fri noon-10pm, Sat 11am-10pm, Sun 11am-9.30pm.

Floridita W1

100 Wardour St   7314 4000   3–2D

A joint venture between the D&D (formerly Conran) empire and a famous bar in Havana, this very large Cuban venue is worth considering if you're looking for a combination of cocktails and spectacle. Shame that the only way to guarantee a table is to dine, though (which, from 7.30pm, attracts a cover charge). There's music from 7.30pm nightly, but, after 9.30pm, drinkers face a £15 entry charge.
/ **Website:** www.floridita.co.uk **Details:** Tue-Wed 5.30pm-2am, Thu-Sat 5.30pm-3am. **Food:** till 1am, Thu-Sat till 3am. **DJ:** nightly.
Live music: 8pm-midnight. **Cover charge may apply.**

Foundry EC2

84-86 Great Eastern St   7739 6900   9–1D

Is it a bar or is it an installation? You never quite know what sort of artifications you're going to find at this grungily-sited former bank branch (which still features a safe in the basement). It's a laid-back, studenty kind of place, but it offers a fair range of booze (with an emphasis on organic lagers), and remains consistently popular. / **Website:** www.foundry.tv
Details: Tue-Sat 4.30pm-11pm, Sun 2.30pm-11pm, closed Mon; no credit cards.

The Fox EC2

28 Paul St   7729 5708   9–1C

This old-fashioned Shoreditch boozer is a welcome antidote to its trendy neighbours, with a cosy, panelled downstairs bar. Upstairs there's an elegant dining room, serving a short menu of notably good British fare. / **Website:** www.thefoxpublichouse.co.uk
Details: Mon-Thu noon-11pm, Fri noon-midnight, Sat 6pm-midnight, Sun noon-6pm; no Amex. **Food:** Mon-Fri L till 3pm, D 6pm-10pm, Sat D only, Sun L only.

The Fox & Anchor EC1

115 Charterhouse St   7250 1300   9–1B

*Breakfast-and-a-pint is an institution at this famous old pub, which – by virtue of its proximity to Smithfield Market – is one of the few licensed to serve from dawn. It was recently given a major revamp, from which its classic Victorian interior emerged magnificently restored, and it nowadays offers an impressive array of whiskies, liqueurs, ales and wines. Good food later in the day too. / **Website:** www.foxandanchor.com* **Details:** *8am-11.30pm.* **Food:** *8am-11am, noon-10pm .*

The Fox & Hounds SW1

29 Passmore St   7730 6367   5–2D

*If you've had enough of ever more chichi Sloane Square, seek out this pocket-handkerchief-size establishment, which – with its cute but hidden corner location – is very much a locals' haunt. It used to be known for its anachronistic licence that prevented it from serving spirits, but these days a G&T is yours for the asking. / **Website:** www.foxandhoundsbelgravia.com* **Details:** *no Amex.* **Food:** *L till 2.30pm, D till 9pm .*

The Fox & Pheasant SW10

1 Billing Rd   7352 2943   5–4A

*For once the name does not lie – this sweet little Greene King pub, (situated in a villagey area between Chelsea and Fulham which estate agents like to call 'The Billings') does feel just like an unpretentious country tavern. With only two small rooms, it's on an intimate scale, and decorated with stuffed creatures and sporting prints. Tiny garden. / **Details:** 11am-midnight; no Amex.* **Food:** *L till 2.30pm.*

Fox Reformed N16

176 Stoke Newington Church St   7254 5975   1–1C

*This sweet, '80s wine bar near the Clissold Park end of Stoke Newington Church Street has long been a favourite local. It offers simple fare and, for the summer, there's a tiny garden. / **Website:** www.fox-reformed.co.uk* **Details:** *Mon-Fri 5pm-midnight, Sat & Sun noon-midnight.* **Food:** *snacks till 11.*

Franklin's SE22

157 Lordship Ln 8299 9598 1–4D

Looking rather like a French-style café, this East Dulwich wine bar (with restaurant behind) is a destination that's particularly popular with local thirty- and fortysomethings who are hunting for a civilised spot in which to down a bottle of vino (or lager). It can get crowded. / **Website:** *www.franklinsrestaurant.com* **Details:** *Mon-Wed noon-11pm, Thu-Sat noon-midnight, Sun noon-11pm.* **Food:** *till 10.30pm.*

Freedom W1

60-66 Wardour St 7437 3490 3–2D

This prominent Soho spot was one of the early wave of trendy bars to hit the area. It remains as popular as ever with a youngish 'rainbow' crowd – this is no longer the mainly gay venue it used to be. On the ground floor, there's a lounge bar offering a wide range of cocktails; in the basement, you'll find "a hedonistic pink fun palace, awash with mirrors, 200 mirror balls, and stunning laser light show", and resident DJs too. / **Website:** *www.freedombarsoho.com* **Details:** *Mon-Thu 5pm-3am, Fri & Sat 2pm-3am, Sun 2pm-11.30pm; no Amex.* **Food:** *till 2am.* **DJ:** *Thu-Sat.* **Cover charge may apply.**

The Freemason's Arms WC2

81-82 Long Acre 7836 3115 4–3C

Located just outside the obvious Covent Garden tourist zone, this large pub – appropriately named, given the proximity of the Masonic Grand Temple – is decorated in a simple but traditional style. As it's a Shepherd Neame operation, it's no surprise that it has quite a strong regular following. Visiting footie boys (and girls), however, may wish to pay their respects to the site where the Football Association was founded, in 1863. / **Food:** *L till 3pm, D till 9pm.*

French House W1

49 Dean St 7437 2477 4–3A

This small and atmospheric Soho freehouse earned its place in history during WWII, when it became a favourite watering hole of de Gaulle and the Free French. It retains a decidedly Gallic air and serves a wide range of aperitifs, French ciders, and a good selection of wines. In recent years, the cosy, upstairs dining room, a separate operation, has developed a name in its own right. / **Website:** *www.frenchhousesoho.com* **Details:** *Mon-Sat noon-11pm, Sun noon-10.30pm.* **Food:** *till 3pm, bar snacks in the evening.*

Freud WC2

198 Shaftesbury Ave   7240 9933   4–1C

*This perennially buzzy cellar bar – established in 1986,
and one of London's first style bars – has always felt like
a 'find'. It barely advertises its presence – look for the fire-
escape stairs in front of the shop of the same name. The décor
makes extensive use of concrete, but it's brightened up by
changing artwork displays.* / **Website:** *www.freudliving.com*
Details: *Sun-Wed 11am-11pm, Thu 11am-1am, Fri 11am-2am,
Sat 11am-1am; no Amex.* **Food:** *L till 4.30pm, bar snacks 6pm-11pm.*

The Fridge Bar SW2

1 Town Hall Pde, Brixton Hill   7326 5100 x103   10–2D

*Next to the famed Brixton club of the same name, this long
and narrow bar/club has a dance-floor downstairs. It's a lively
place, with DJs playing a range of music from hip-hop to house,
and attracts a diverse crowd. Late opening (sometimes until the
following day) is a key attraction.* / **Website:** *www.fridgebar.com*
Details: *Mon-Fri 8pm-4am, closed Sat & Sun; no Amex.* **DJ:** *Fri-Mon.*
Live music: *nightly.* **Cover charge may apply.**

G-A-Y Bar W1

30 Old Compton St   7494 2756   4–2A

*This well-known, three-floor Soho 'video bar' offers the tried-
and-trusted formula of heavily marked-up beers, beefy bar staff
and standing-room only at weekends. Like its sibling club night
at the Astoria, it's long on high-octane campness – definitely
a shirts-off kind of place.* / **Website:** *www.g-a-y.co.uk*
Details: *noon-midnight; no Amex.* **Food:** *bar snacks till midnight.*
Happy hour: *Sun-Thu.*

Galvin at Windows
Park Lane Hilton W1

22 Park Ln   7208 4021   3–4A

*Wow! What a view! You can see why the Queen wasn't keen
on the Park Lane Hilton being built, back in the early-'60s,
when you look down from its 28th-floor bar, right in to her back
garden. (To this day, she has never set foot in the place.)
Nowadays it's run by the Galvin brothers, who also run the
swanky neighbouring restaurant. No bargain, obviously,
but undoubtedly a special destination.*
/ **Website:** *www.galvinatwindows.com* **Details:** *Mon-Wed 10am-1am, Thu-Sat
10am-3am, Sun 10am-10.30pm.* **Food:** *Mon-Wed till 12.30am, Thu-Fri till
2.30am, Sat till 2.30am, Sun till 10.30pm.* **Cover charge may apply.**

Garlic & Shots W1

14 Frith St   7734 9505   4–2A

An offshoot of an outfit in Stockholm, this Soho curiosity is certainly a London one-off – in the upstairs restaurant, all the food (ice cream included) comes laced with garlic. Drinkswise (there's also a cellar bar and hidden, little garden) the speciality is a choice of a hundred vodkas. Why is it no surprise that Goths and metallers predominate?
/ Website: www.garlicandshots.com Details: Mon-Wed 5pm-midnight, Thu-Sat 6pm-1am, Sun 5pm-11.30pm; no Amex. Food: till 11.15pm, Fri & Sat till 12.15am.

The Garrison SE1

99-101 Bermondsey St   7089 9355   9–4D

This tightly-packed gastropub, near Bermondsey Antiques Market, is an ever-buzzing place, largely devoted to dining. It's a quirky sort of establishment, where the food is often very good. Got a film to show? In the basement, there's a screening room for rent. / Website: www.thegarrison.co.uk Details: Mon-Sat 8am-11pm, Sun 9am-10.30pm. Food: L&D.

The George & Dragon E2

2 Hackney Rd   7012 1100   9–1D

Kitsch, retro décor and a juke box and DJ spinning boppy hits from the '70s and '80s helps create a good-natured atmosphere at this often-packed pub, in 'Hoxditch'. It's a gay-friendly joint, but the crowd can be quite mixed.
/ Details: 6pm-11pm. DJ: nightly.

George Inn SE1

77 Borough High St   7407 2056   9–4C

London's sole surviving galleried 17th-century coaching inn, off a cobbled courtyard near London Bridge, is owned by the National Trust. Its bars and panelled drinking rooms were allegedly haunts of both Samuel Johnson and Shakespeare – as well as being mentioned by Dickens – so expect a year-round tourist crush. / Website: www.functionroomslondon.co.uk Details: Mon-Sat 11am-11pm, Sun 11am-10.30pm. Food: noon-9pm (6pm at weekends).

George IV W4

185 Chiswick High Rd   8994 4624   7–2A

This large Fullers tavern is one of the more prominent features of Chiswick's main drag. With its rambling interior and cute courtyard, it makes a nice enough place to drink, but for a really entertaining evening the star feature is its 'Headliners' comedy venue (entry charge applies). / Website: - Details: Mon-Thu 11.30am-11pm, Fri & Sat 11.30am-1am, Sun noon-11pm . Food: Mon-Sat till 10pm, Sun till 7pm.

Gilgamesh NW1

The Stables Camden Mkt   7482 5757   8–2B

It took many man-years of Indian craftsmanship to create the mind-boggling, carved-wood interior of this epic bar/restaurant, located above Camden Market. The large, low-ceilinged cocktail bar makes an OK stand-alone destination, but the place is actually best if you're also eating (as the pricey pan-Asian food is not bad, and the restaurant is the venue's most impressive space). / Website: www.gilgameshbar.com Details: Mon-Thu noon-3pm, 6pm-3am, Fri-Sun noon-3am. Food: till 12.30am. DJ: Fri-Sun. Cover charge may apply.

Gilt Champagne Lounge
Jumeirah Carlton Tower SW1

Cadogan Pl   7858 7250   5–1D

A handy place to know about in ever-trendier Belgravia – the bling-y cocktail bar at this contemporary, but essentially traditional, grand hotel, five minutes' walk from Harrods. / Website: www.jumeirahcarltontower.com/dining/gilt Details: Mon-Sat 5pm-3am, Sun 5pm-11pm .

Ginglik W12

1 Shepherd's Bush Gn   8749 2310   7–1C

To say everyone was gobsmacked when Robin Williams turned up one night unannounced to do stand-up at these subterranean former WC at the tip of Shepherd's Bush Green is something of an understatement. It's a measure, though, of the ongoing success of this endearingly quirky venue. It bills itself as a 'beat bunker', but also features regular comedy and film nights. / Website: www.ginglik.co.uk Details: Mon-Thu 7pm-1am, Fri & Sat 7pm-3am, Sun 7pm-12.30am. Food: always available. DJ: Some Fridays and every Sat. Live music: nightly. Cover charge may apply.

Goat In Boots SW10

333 Fulham Rd   7352 1384   5–3B

Long before anyone called the strip of road it occupies the 'Beach', it was trendy for younger folk to laze around in – or, more especially, outside – this Chelsea boozer, and it remains a key venue for the local gilded youth. Upstairs, there's a club – "333". / **Details:** *Mon-Thu noon-midnight, Fri & Sat noon-1am; no Amex.* **DJ:** *Sat.*

The Golden Heart E1

110 Commercial St   7247 2158   9–1D

If it wasn't for its location (near Spitalfields Market), this large pub would be a classic East End boozer (complete with dog), overseen for 30 years by one landlady (Sandra Esqulant). As is, it's now also a social melting pot throwing together long-time regulars with the trendies who have colonised the 'hood – most famously Tracy Emin and her BritArt cronies. / **Details:** *Mon-Sat 11am-midnight, Sun 11am-10.30pm.*

Gordon's Wine Bar WC2

47 Villiers St   7930 1408   2–2D

London's oldest wine bar – in wonderfully gloomy candlelit cellars near Embankment tube – is accessed via an anonymous doorway, down a set of rickety stairs. It offers a good range of wines (plus sherries, ports and Madeiras, but nothing else) at tolerable prices, plus rather expensive hot dishes and plates of cheese. In summer, arrive early to bag a prized table on one of the nicest terraces in the centre of town. / **Website:** *www.gordonswinebar.com* **Details:** *Mon-Fri 10am-11pm, Sat 11am-11pm, Sun noon-10pm; no Amex.* **Food:** *till 10pm.*

Goring Hotel SW1

15 Beeston Pl   7396 9000   2–4B

An elegant drinking experience within two minutes of Victoria Station is not the impossible dream you might think, at least not if you seek out the bar of the hotel that's been in the Goring family for almost a century. A walk on the wild side it is not, but, if it's traditional comfort and civilisation you're after, few places in town equal its calm and attention to detail. / **Website:** *www.goringhotel.co.uk* **Details:** *7am-11pm.* **Food:** *till 11pm.*

The Gowlett SE15

62 Gowlett Rd 7635 7048 1–4C

A Peckham success-story. This top local manages an all-too-rare combination of simple things done well. Unusually for a pub, this includes cracking pizza, but there's also a constantly changing selection of ales that would do any beer-bore proud, well-chosen wines, regular live music and an ever-changing selection of works by local artists. And you can happily take the kids. / **Website:** www.thegowlett.com **Details:** Mon-Thu noon-midnight, Fri & Sat noon-1am, Sun noon-11.30pm. **Food:** Mon-Fri L 12.30pm-2.30pm, D 6.30pm-10.30pm, Sat 12.30pm-10.30pm, Sun 12.30pm-9pm. **DJ:** Sun. **Live music:** pianist last Wed of every month.

Grafton House SW4

13-19 Old Town 7498 5559 10–1D

It may have rather barn-like proportions, but this Clapham Old Town bar — with a spacious restaurant at the rear — has made itself a very popular rendezvous with younger locals. It now boasts a nicely designed beer garden too. / **Website:** www.graftonhouseuk.com **Details:** Mon-Wed noon-11pm, Thu noon-1am, Fri & Sat 10am-1am, Sun noon-11pm. **Food:** L till 4pm D 7-11. **DJ:** Fri & Sat. **Live music:** Thu.

La Grande Marque EC4

47 Ludgate Hill 7329 6709 9–2A

A grand (and listed) Victorian bank building — with an impressive interior more evocative of Vienna than London — provides the setting for this superior wine bar, just down the hill from St Paul's. Champagne is quite a house speciality, but Bitburger lager is also available. / **Website:** www.lagrandemarque.co.uk **Details:** Mon-Fri 11am-11pm, closed Sat & Sun. **Food:** L till 3pm, afternoon snacks.

The Grapes E14

76 Narrow St 7987 4396 11–1B

For our money the nicest of the historic East End riverside taverns, this quiet and characterful little pub (established 1583, rebuilt 1720) is a nice, no-nonsense place whose remote location (near the Limehouse Link) thankfully keeps it off the tourist trail. Fish 'n' chips in the bar would be a great accompaniment to a pint of Adnams. Or eat in the more formal seafood restaurant upstairs, which boasts impressive river views. No children. / **Details:** Mon-Wed noon-3pm, 5.30pm-11pm, Thu-Sat noon-11pm, Sun noon-10.30pm; no Amex. **Food:** till 9.30pm.

Great Eastern Dining Room EC2

54-56 Great Eastern St   7613 4545   9–1D

*It was at this Shoreditch bar/restaurant that Will Ricker, now of Notting Hill's 'E&O' fame, began to make his name. The place attracts a mature crowd by local standards, drawn by a combination of sophisticated styling and original cocktails. Downstairs, in 'Below 54', the music is louder and the style more clubby. Food, Asian in inspiration, is a major part of the operation. / **Website:** www.greateasterndining.co.uk **Details:** Mon-Fri noon-midnight, Sat 6pm-midnight, closed Sun. **Food:** till midnight. **DJ:** Fri & Sat.*

Green & Blue SE22

38 Lordship Ln   8693 9250   1–4D

*An oenophiles' delight, this East Dulwich bar allows you the opportunity to sample the list of a small wine merchant that Decanter magazine, no less, has proclaimed the UK's best of its type. If you wish, simple meals are available by way of accompaniment or, for a small fee, you can even BYO — food that is! / **Website:** www.greenandbluewines.com **Details:** Mon-Fri 9am-11pm, Sat 9am-midnight, Sun 11am-10.30pm; no Amex. **Food:** till 1 hour before closing.*

Green & Red E1

51 Bethnal Green Rd   7749 9670   1–2D

*"The vibrancy of Mexico, without the usual sombrero and stuffed donkey Mexicana" — that's the promise of this easy-going but stylish hang-out near the top of Brick Lane, and it fully delivers. Leaving aside the excellent food — from snacks to a substantial meal — the well-stocked bar includes the largest collection of tequilas in the country. / **Website:** www.greenred.co.uk **Details:** Mon-Thu 5.30pm-midnight, Fri & Sat 5.30pm-1am, Sun 5.30pm-10.30pm. **Food:** taco stand on weekends, bar snacks available. **DJ:** Fri-Sat.*

Green Carnation W1

5 Greek St   7434 3323   4–2A

*The opulent upstairs — a homage to Oscar Wilde, with dark green wallpaper, a huge fireplace, oils and mirrors — is the high point at this classy gay outfit in Soho. In the downstairs bar, there's the usual DJ and dancing, but not the decadent distinctiveness you find above. / **Website:** www.greencarnationsoho.co.uk **Details:** Mon-Sat 4pm-2am, Sun 4pm-midnight. **Food:** 7pm-10pm. **DJ:** Tue, Thu-Sat 9pm. **Live music:** Mon, Wed, Thu, Sat. **Happy hour:** 4pm-7pm. **Cover charge** may apply.*

The Grenadier SW1

18 Wilton Rw   7235 3074   5–1D

A storybook-perfect mews location contributes to the enormous popularity of this cute and ancient tavern, a stone's throw from Hyde Park Corner. It's in all the tourist guides and often packed to the rafters, but somehow manages to retain its charm. There is a tiny restaurant, but those in the know settle for a Bloody Mary and a sausage at the bar. No children (unless dining).
*/ **Food:** L till 2.30pm, D till 9pm.*

Ground Floor W11

186 Portobello Rd   7243 0072   6–1A

*When Notting Hill was starting to turn trendy at the end of the '80s, this sofa-strewn lounge bar was one of the first places to be converted from a terrifyingly gritty boozer into a cool hang-out for the growing ranks of Notting Hillbillies. You'd be hard pressed to tell it from many other modern bars these days, but vestiges of its glamorous past linger. And, yes, it was in The Film. / **Website:** www.firstfloorportobello.co.uk*
***Details:** noon-midnight. **Food:** till 10pm. **DJ:** Sun & Thu.*

Guanabara WC2

Parker St   7242 8600   4–1D

Named after Rio de Janeiro's bay, this huge Brazilian-themed venue (in the New London Theatre) brings a fair amount of Latino vibrancy to the fringes of Covent Garden. Regular DJs and live music are much of the attraction, plus South American tapas to soak up the cocktails and fruit caipirinhas.
*/ **Website:** www.guanabara.co.uk **Details:** Mon-Sat 5pm-2.30am, Sun 5pm-midnight. **Food:** till 11pm. **DJ & Live music:** nightly. **Happy hour:** Mon-Thu 5pm-7.30pm, Fri & Sat 5pm-7pm. **Cover charge may apply.***

The Guinea W1

30 Bruton Pl   7409 1728   3–2B

The tail rather wags the dog at this Young's tavern, hidden away in a pretty Mayfair mews – the bar is dwarfed in scale by the restaurant. Still, it makes a characterful, traditional spot for a pint of ale and, if you have a big appetite and a gold card, the steaks served next door are pretty good too.
*/ **Website:** www.theguinea.co.uk **Details:** Mon-Fri 11.30am-11pm, Sat 6pm-11pm, closed Sun. **Food:** L till 3pm, D till 10.30pm.*

The Gun E14

27 Coldharbour   7515 5222   11–1C

Occupying an impressive waterside 18th-century building, Tom and Ed Martin's hugely popular gastropub is within walking distance of Canary Wharf, and has a great view of the O2, across the river. As well as a good selection of beers and an extensive wine list, there's also a good-but-pricey range of dining options (including a Portuguese barbecue).
/ **Website:** www.thegundocklands.com **Details:** Mon-Sat 11am-midnight, Sun 11am-11pm. **Food:** L Mon-Fri noon-3pm Sat-Sun noon-4pm; D Mon-Sat 6pm-10.30pm, Sun 6pm-9.30pm.

Hakkasan W1

8 Hanway Pl   7927 7000   4–1A

Despite its grungy location, off Tottenham Court Road, this beautifully-designed oriental basement bar/restaurant has been a smash hit with a chic (and necessarily prosperous) thirtysomething crowd. The cocktail bar is only a small part of the whole, but it's a high-quality operation which makes a cool spot to hang out, and you can dine from the (relatively) inexpensive bar menu. / **Details:** Mon-Wed noon-12.30am, Thu-Sat noon-1.30am, Sun noon-midnight. **Food:** always available. **DJ:** nightly.

Half Moon SW15

93 Lower Richmond Rd   8780 9383   10–1B

A ten-minute walk from Putney Bridge, this large and nicely seedy Young's boozer is one of the better-known music pubs in the capital (having hosted Van Morrison, the Stones, U2 and Kate Bush). Performances take place in the grotty rear room, but there's also quite a lot going on in the characterful front bar, which attracts a diverse clientele.
/ **Website:** www.halfmoon.co.uk **Details:** Mon-Thu noon-11.30pm, Fri & Sat noon-midnight, Sun noon-11pm; no Amex. **Cover charge may apply.**

Hare & Billet SE3

1A, Hare & Billet Rd   8852 2352   1–4D

Not only is this the oldest pub in Blackheath, but it's also one of the most consistently popular. It offers a fair range of beers and satisfying food, plus nice views of the heath.
/ **Details:** Sun-Thu 11am-11pm, Fri & Sat 11am-midnight. **Food:** Mon-Fri till 9pm, Sat & Sun till 7.30pm.

Harrisons SW12

15-19 Bedford Hill   8675 6900   10–2C

Formerly called the Balham Bar & Grill (when it was under the same fashionable umbrella as 'Soho House'), this smart but informal neighbourhood spot remains, by the standards of the area, a glamorous destination for a drink. (You can eat here too, but its attractions on that score are much less evident).
/ **Website:** www.harrisonsbalham.co.uk **Details:** Sun-Thu noon-midnight, Fri & Sat noon-1am. **Food:** till 10.30pm.

The Hartley SE1

64 Tower Bridge Rd   7394 7023   9–4D

A mile or so south of Tower Bridge, this 'bar & dining room' offers a useful amenity in an area without much in the way of competition. Hearty (often organic) meat dishes are a highlight of the no-nonsense menu. It's also by far the most civilised place to drink hereabouts, and its 'offer' includes a fair range of reasonably-priced wines.
/ **Website:** www.thehartley.com **Details:** Mon-Fri noon-11pm, Sat & Sun 11am-11pm. **Food:** till 10pm, Sun till 6pm.

Harwood Arms SW6

Walham Grove   7386 1847   5–3A

In recent years, it has always been welcome surprise for first-timers to stumble across this cheerful backstreet boozer, lost in the maze of roads north of Fulham Broadway. Since a new team arrived in late-2008, however, it has quickly acquired a big reputation for the quality of its very English cuisine, but it remains a congenial destination for those just in search of a drink. / **Details:** Sun-Thu noon-11pm, Fri & Sat noon-midnight, closed Mondays. **Food:** L till 3pm, D till 9.30pm.

The Havelock Tavern W14

57 Masbro Rd   7603 5374   7–1C

The popularity of this famous gastropub is inversely proportional to the obscurity of its Olympia backstreet location (or the infamously off-hand attitude of its staff). Despite its foodie credentials, though, this is still a good place just for a pint. Arrive early if you want a table.
/ **Website:** www.thehavelocktavern.co.uk **Details:** Mon-Sat 11am-11pm, Sun noon-10.30pm. **Food:** L noon-2.30pm, D 7pm till 10pm.

The Hawksmoor E1

157 Commercial St   7247 7392   9–1D

You don't have to like steak (though it does help) to visit this loudly buzzing, brick-walled bar/restaurant, just to the north of Spitalfields Market. If you're not in the mood for a hearty meat-fest, however, the magnificent cocktails are an attraction in themselves. / Website: www.thehawksmoor.co.uk Details: Mon-Sat noon-midnight, Sun 6pm-midnight. Food: L till 4.30pm, D till 10.30pm.

Heights Bar
St George's Hotel W1

Langham Pl   7580 0111   3–1C

While the vista falls short of being truly amazing, there's only so little you can see from the 15th floor of a central London building – the view certainly lends a sense of occasion to a trip to this cocktail lounge, atop a '60s hotel, by Broadcasting House. / Website: www.saintgeorgeshotel.com Details: Mon-Sat 7am-midnight, Sun 7am-11pm. Food: till 10pm. Happy hour: 5pm-6pm.

The Hemingford Arms N1

158 Hemingford Rd   7607 3303   8–2D

On a quiet Barnsbury corner, this neighbourhood pub (part of the excellent Capital Pub Company) is the kind of superior local anyone would be pleased to have at the end of the road. It has a cosy Victorian interior enlivened with a fair amount of bric-a-brac, and offers a good selection of ales on tap, and regular live music. / Website: www.capitalpubcompany.com/hemingford Details: Mon-Sat 11am-11pm, Sun noon-10.30pm. Food: Mon-Fri noon-3pm, Tue-Sun 6pm-10.30pm, Sun noon-5pm.

Henry J Beans SW3

195 King's Rd   7352 9255   5–3C

Beer, burgers and cocktails on an American theme are what this "bar & grill" chain is all about. The Chelsea branch listed is of particular note – not because of the interior (which is typically themey), nor its fare, but because of the huge and attractive (and completely unexpected) garden, which draws a real crowd on sunny days. / Website: www.henryjbeans.com Details: Mon-Thu 11am-11pm, Fri & Sat 11am-midnight, Sun noon-midnight. Food: till 10.30pm. DJ: Fri & Sat.

The Hillgate Arms W8

24 Hillgate St   7727 8543   6–2B
*Hillgate Village – as estate agents call the little enclave
just south of Notting Hill Gate – is, in its quiet way, one of the
cutest spots in town. At its heart, this pretty boozer is one
of those rare civilised traditional pubs, and it's regularly crowded
with well-heeled locals, cinema-goers and so on. There are
a few seats outside. / Website: www.innventiveoperations.com*
Details: *Mon-Sat 11am-11pm, Sun noon-10.30pm; no Amex.* **Food:** *till 9pm.*

The Holly Bush NW3

22 Holly Mount   7435 2892   8–1A
*This 18th-century tavern is pretty much unchanged by the
passing of the years (well, OK, the gas-lighting has been
adapted to electric), and enjoys one of the most picturesque
locations in London – in a warren of streets and walkways, up a
stone staircase from Hampstead's Heath Street. On a summer
day, drinkers annex the pavement outside.
/ Website: www.hollybushpub.com* **Details:** *Mon-Sat noon-11pm,
Sun noon-10.30pm; no Amex.* **Food:** *till 10pm, Sun till 9pm.*

Holy Drinker SW11

59 Northcote Rd   7801 0544   10–2C
*Intimate lighting, chilled music, candles and a brace of open
fires contribute much to the atmosphere of this Battersea bar,
which has been quite a success with the local Bohemians. The
array of drinks is impressive, and includes 30 ales and lagers,
as well as a good wine selection. / Website: www.holydrinker.co.uk*
Details: *Mon-Wed 4.30pm-11pm, Thu & Fri 4.30pm-midnight,
Sat noon-midnight, Sun 1pm-11pm; no Amex.* **DJ:** *Fri & Sat 8pm-midnight.*

Home EC2

100-106 Leonard St   7684 8618   9–1C
*When it opened (then just occupying the basement) in 1997,
this funky bar/restaurant was the coolest thing ever to have hit
the East End (and back then, you ate in a cellar, not upstairs
like now). Nowadays it's no longer at the cutting edge, but that's
not to say it's no good – it's an easygoing loungy hang-out which
gets louder later in the week, when the regular DJs crank
up the volume. / Website: www.homebar.co.uk* **Details:** *Mon-Wed
5pm-midnight, Thu-Fri 5pm-2am, Sat 7pm-2am closed Sun.* **Food:** *noon-3pm,
6pm-10pm (11pm Thu-Sat).* **DJ:** *Thu-Sat.*

Hope & Anchor N1

207 Upper St   7354 1312   8–2D

DJs and live bands provide music nightly (until 1am), at this darkly-revamped Greene King boozer in Islington, in the basement of which many of the big names of New Wave and Punk – The Clash, The Stranglers, The Cure – cut their musical teeth. Upstairs, you can play pool or table football.
/ **Details:** *Mon-Wed noon-11pm, Thu-Sat noon-1am, Sun noon-10.30pm; no Amex.* **Food:** *Mon-Sat till 5pm, no food Sun.* **DJ:** *Thu-Sat.*
Live music: *Mon-Sun.* **Cover charge may apply.**

Horse SE1

124 Westminster Bridge Rd   7928 6277   2–3D

The area around Lambeth North tube is not especially rich in nice places to drink (or eat), so the oddly-named revamp of this atmospheric old boozer was good news locally. It makes a pleasant place for a pint or a glass of wine, and Thai food is also available. No children. / **Website:** *www.horsebar.co.uk*
Details: *Mon-Thu noon-11.30pm, Fri noon-midnight, Sat 6pm-midnight, closed Sun.* **Food:** *L till 3pm, D till 10pm.*

The Hoxton Grille
Hoxton Urban Lounge EC2

81 Great Eastern St   7739 9111   9–1D

Much of the ground floor of this Hoxton hotel is taken up with a loungy bar and brasserie space, so – except at very busy times – this makes an unusually comfortable and relaxed place for a drink. Lucky winter drinkers may secure a perch by the fire. / **Website:** *www.grillerestaurants.com* **Details:** *Mon-Fri 8.30pm-midnight, closed Sat & Sun.* **Food:** *Mon-Tue & Sun till 10.30pm, Wed-Sat till 11pm.*

The Hoxton Pony EC2

104-108 Curtain Rd   7613 2844   9–1D

On the site that was once Pool (RIP), this stylish recent arrival – owned by the son of legendary mixologist Salvatore Calabrese – exudes a level of glamour unusual for the immediate area. Upstairs is a long modern bar with an emphasis on cocktails (and food from the open kitchen), while downstairs there's a DJ and a small dance floor. / **Website:** *www.thehoxtonpony.com*
Details: *Mon-Thu noon-1am, Fri noon-2am, Sat 6.30pm-2am, Sun open for special events.* **Food:** *Mon-Fri noon-10pm.* **DJ:** *Thu-Sat.*

Hoxton Square Bar & Kitchen N1

2-4 Hoxton Sq   7613 0709   9–1D
It's not just a location on the square itself which makes this large bar a key Hoxton destination. Bare concrete décor is softened by subdued lighting and a cool crowd lounging on the plentiful supply of sofas. Music stretches from reggae to heavy metal, but usually at a volume where conversation is feasible. The pleasant terrace is a prime summer posing spot.
/ **Website:** www.hoxtonsquarebar.com **Details:** Mon 11am-midnight, Tue-Thu 11am-1am, Fri & Sat 11am-2am. **Food:** till 11pm. **DJ:** Fri-Sun.

Hush W1

8 Lancashire Ct   7659 1500   3–2B
A quiet courtyard, just off Bond Street, makes a perfect, smart location for this expensively trendy bar (plus brasserie and restaurant), which is typically packed with a perma-tanned crowd that would look equally at home in St Tropez or Verbier.
/ **Website:** www.hush.co.uk **Details:** Mon-Sat 11am-11pm, closed Sun.
Food: till 11pm.

Island W2

Lancaster Ter   7551 6070   6–2D
It's mainly a restaurant, but, after a walk in Hyde Park, this striking contemporary addition to the Bayswater townscape makes a classy cocktail destination. Indeed, as the owners seem to have put more thought into the architecture of the double-height interior than they have to the cooking, this is arguably a place of more interest to drinkers than it is to diners.
/ **Website:** www.islandrestaurant.co.uk **Details:** Mon-Sat noon-10.45pm, Sun noon-10.30pm. **Food:** till 10.30pm.

Itsu SW3

118 Draycott Ave   7584 5522   5–2C
This is just a popular branch of the sushi-conveyor chain, right? Well not just, actually. If you're shopping at nearby Brompton Cross, it is worth knowing about its 'surprise' bar, hidden-away upstairs, which can be a handy spot for a quick snifter.
/ **Website:** www.itsu.co.uk **Details:** Mon-Sat noon-11pm, Sun noon-10pm.
Food: till 11pm .

Jamaica Wine House EC3

St Michael's Alley   7929 6972   9–2C

A sensitive revamp (by the 'Tup' people) didn't destroy the anachronistic appeal of this back alley bastion of olde London (on the site of the City's first coffee house). It serves a good range of lagers and bitters, and there's also quite an emphasis on wine. / **Website:** www.innventiveoperations.com **Details:** *closed Sat & Sun.* **Food:** *till 3pm.*

Jerusalem W1

33-34 Rathbone Pl   7255 1120   3–1D

Just north of Oxford Street, this candlelit basement bar has an ecclesiastical feel, with long tables and old church pews. After half a decade in business, it remains quite a destination, thanks in part to its DJs, who play – depending on the night – a mixture of dance, house & Latino funk. / **Website:** www.fabbars.com **Details:** *Mon noon-11pm, Tue-Wed noon-midnight, Thu-Sat 7pm-1am, closed Sun.* **Food:** *till 10pm .* **DJ:** *Thu-Sat.* **Cover charge may apply.**

The Jerusalem Tavern EC1

55 Britton St   7490 4281   9–1A

The sole London outpost of a highly respected Suffolk brewery – St Peter's – this tiny Clerkenwell bar (dating back to 1720) is an ale-lover's paradise, and a charming spot in which to while away a few hours. All of the company's (excellent) cask and bottled ales are available, from the light Golden Ale to the old-style Porter. Bar snacks at lunchtime. / **Website:** www.stpetersbrewery.co.uk **Details:** *Mon-Fri 11am-11pm, closed Sat & Sun.* **Food:** *Mon-Fri L till 3pm, Tue-Thu-D 10pm.*

Jugged Hare SW1

172 Vauxhall Bridge Rd   7828 1543   2–4B

A grand former bank building provides the impressive setting for this ornately decorated Fullers pub. It might not be the best boozer in the world, but if you're looking for a place within a few minutes' walk of Victoria station, it is one of the more congenial. / **Website:** www.fullers.co.uk **Details:** *Mon-Thu, Sat 11am-11pm, Fri 11am-11.30pm, Sun noon-10.30.* **Food:** *till 9.30pm.*

Julie's Bar W11

135 Portland Rd   7727 7985   6–2A

With its lavish and eclectic décor, this long-established Holland Park wine bar (next to Julie's restaurant) is one of the most enduringly popular in town. It's a comfortable and characterful place with a nice terrace, all of which helps to justify its rather hefty prices (especially for the food). Wine, and particularly champagne, is the tipple of choice, but there's also a selection of cocktails. / Website: www.juliesrestaurant.com **Details:** *Mon-Sat 9am-11.30pm, Sun 9am-11pm.* **Food:** *till 10.45pm, Sun till 10.15pm.*

Just Oriental SW1

19 King St   7976 2222   3–4D

Apart from the style of the snacks on offer, there's not really much oriental about this cocktail bar, in the basement below the Just St. James restaurant. It is, however, well worth knowing about as one of the more spacious and comfortable bars around St James's, and it has always been younger in appeal than many other places in that stuffy part of town. / Website: www.juststjames.com **Details:** *Mon-Fri noon-1am, Sat 6pm-1am, closed Sun.* **Food:** *till 11pm.*

Keston Lodge N1

131 Upper St   7354 9535   8–3D

This funked-up former All Bar One – now got up in panelled, shabby-chic style, and with plenty of comfy sofas – has been quite a hit with Islington hipsters. There's also a food operation (pies a speciality), which helps make the place a useful stand-by at any time of day. / Website: www.kestonlodge.com **Details:** *Mon-Wed noon-midnight, Thu noon-1am, Fri & Sat noon-3am, Sun noon-11.30pm ; no Amex.* **Food:** *L noon-4pm, D 6pm-10.00pm.* **DJ:** *Thu-Sun.* **Happy hour:** *cocktail promotion 5pm-7pm daily.* **Cover charge** *may apply.*

Kettners W1

29 Romilly St   7734 6112 · 4–2A

This vast, characterful Soho landmark (founded in 1867 by a former chef of Napoleon III) has been best known in recent years as a grand pizzeria, but has always also had this ground-floor champagne bar. The whole building was prettified and relaunched in late-2008 as a Gallic café/brasserie. The classy bar survives and is arguably still the most attractive part of the operation. / Website: www.kettners.com **Details:** *8am-1am.* **Food:** *B 8am-11.30am, L 11.30am-3pm, D 5pm-1am.*

King's Head N1

115 Upper St   7226 4443   8–2D

Very fine and very Victorian, this superbly unmucked-about-with hostelry is an unchanging fixture in Islington's ever-changing pub scene. The lofty ground-floor bar has regular live music and a pleasant, slightly student feel. To the rear, what is claimed to be London's oldest pub-theatre (tel 7226 1916) often puts on critically acclaimed performances.
/ **Website:** www.kingsheadtheatre.org **Details:** Mon-Thu 11am-1am, Fri & Sat 11am-2am, Sun noon-12.30am; no Amex. **DJ:** Fri. **Live music:** Wed & Sun. **Happy hour:** 5pm-7pm.

Kudos WC2

10 Adelaide St   7379 4573   2–3C

A minute from Trafalgar Square, this chilled gay(ish) bar on two levels has attracted a diverse crowd for over a decade. The ground floor has a glass frontage (which is opened completely during summer) so the boyz can check you out checking them out. Downstairs is slightly more intimate, with alcoves, low lighting and video screens. / **Details:** Mon-Fri 4pm-midnight, Sat 2pm-midnight, Sun 2pm-11pm. **DJ:** Fri & Sat.

Lab W1

12 Old Compton St   7437 7820   4–2A

The London Academy of Bartending, no less. As you'd expect, flashy 'mixology' is taken seriously at this retro Soho spot, and an impressive tome lists the resulting cocktails, from classics to 'visionaries' (and even 'experiments'). There's a second bar downstairs, with regular DJs.
/ **Website:** www.lab-townhouse.com **Details:** Mon-Sat 4pm-midnight, Sun 4pm-10.30pm. **Food:** Mon-Sat till midnight, Sun till 10.30pm. **DJ:** Mon-Sat.

The Ladbroke Arms W11

54 Ladbroke Rd   7727 6648   6–2B

This excellent, hidden-away pub, a short walk from Notting Hill Gate, is a cosy and welcoming place, with a particular reputation for its food, and a good choice of wines too. Despite its quiet side-street location, it's busy enough at the best of times, and especially so in summer when the small but very nice terrace is full to overflowing.
/ **Website:** www.ladbrokearms.com **Details:** Mon-Sat 11.30am-11pm, Sun noon-10.30pm. **Food:** L till 2.30pm (weekends till 3pm), D till 9.30pm.

The Lamb WC1

94 Lamb's Conduit St   7405 0713   2–1D

Just south of Coram's Fields in Bloomsbury, this Young's pub is the epitome of a friendly, cosy, traditional, no-nonsense place. Attractions include a particularly fine Victorian interior (with snob screens still in situ) and a rear terrace.
/ Website: www.youngs.co.uk Details: Mon-Sat 11am-midnight, Sun noon-10.30pm. Food: till 9pm.

The Lamb & Flag WC2

33 Rose St   7497 9504   4–3C

This ancient (late-17th century) and extremely atmospheric Covent Garden tavern couldn't really be much more central, and it's hugely popular as a West End rendezvous. It has a particularly nice small courtyard at the front, which is full to bursting on sunny days. / Details: no Amex. Food: till 3pm.
Happy hour: Mon-Fri 11am-5pm.

The Lamb Tavern EC3

10-12 Leadenhall Mkt   7626 2454   9–3D

With a splendid location at the heart of a magnificent covered Victorian market, this Young's operation is one of the City's better traditional pubs. Inside there are a number of rooms, including an elegant first-floor dining room and a basement wine bar with impressive Edwardian tiles. Or drink 'outside' in the market. / Website: www.thelambtavern.co.uk Details: Mon-Fri 11am-11pm, closed Sat & Sun. Food: L noon-3 D 6pm-10pm.

The Library
Lanesborough Hotel SW1

1 Lanesborough Pl, Hyde Pk Corner   7259 5599   5–1D

The rich interior of this landmark hotel's bar has a sumptuousness that puts most St James's clubs to shame. If you're really looking to spend spend spend, it features one of the capital's most comprehensive range of aged cognacs.
/ Website: www.lanesborough.com Details: Mon-Sat 11am-1am, Sun noon-10.30pm. Food: till midnight.

The Langley WC2

5 Langley St   7836 5005   4–2C

Early in the week, these retro cellars tucked away in Covent Garden make a handy spot for a truly central rendezvous. Closer to the weekend, however, you'll have difficulty hearing yourself talk (let alone getting in), as crowds of frenzied office guys 'n' gals apply themselves to the serious task of getting plastered on happy hour cocktails. / **Website:** *www.thelangley.co.uk* **Details:** *Mon-Sat 4.30pm-1am, Sun 4pm-10.30pm.* **Food:** *till 11pm, Sun till 10.30pm.* **DJ:** *Thu-Sat.* **Happy hour:** *Mon-Sun 5pm-8pm.* **Cover charge may apply.**

Lansdowne NW1

90 Gloucester Ave   7483 0409   8–3B

Like its nearby rival The Engineer (which it pre-dated by a few months), this chilled gastropub is one of the mainstays of Primrose Hill life, and always attracts quite a crowd. The cooking is on a par with what you get down the road (the selection of pizza here being the top tip). / **Website:** *www.thelansdownepub.co.uk* **Details:** *Mon-Fri noon-11pm, Sat 9.30am-11pm, Sun 9.30am-10.30pm; no Amex.* **Food:** *L till 3pm, D till 10pm.*

The Light E1

233 Shoreditch High St   7247 8989   9–1D

Stylishly converted from an electricity station (recently saved from demolition), this airy and buzzy bar/restaurant, just north of Liverpool Street, offers a refreshing change from the ubiquitous chain bars and dreary boozers of the locality. It is very popular for post-work drinks. School dinner-style bar snacks or a meal in the adjoining restaurant help soak up the booze. / **Website:** *www.thelightE1.com* **Details:** *Mon-Wed noon-midnight, Thu & Fri noon-2am, Sat 6.30pm-2am, Sun noon-10.30pm.* **Food:** *till 10.30pm.* **DJ:** *Thu-Sat.*

Light Bar
St Martin's Lane Hotel WC2

St Martin's Ln, Covent Garden   7300 5599   4–3C

Like its cousin at the Sanderson (The Long Bar, see also), this Ian Schrager design-hotel – his original London venture – combines groovy Philippe Starck styling with a fashionista reputation. Unless you're staying in the hotel, you're well-advised to call ahead and get yourself on the guest list. / **Website:** *www.stmartinslane.com* **Details:** *Mon-Sat 5.30pm-3am, Sun 5.30pm-midnight .* **DJ:** *Thu-Sat.*

The Lock Tavern NW1

35 Chalk Farm Rd   7482 7163   8–2B

This long and thin bar/café is a short walk from Chalk Farm tube, and atmospherically decorated with dark wood and ornate mirrors. An open kitchen at the back dispenses food – if the roaring trade they do at lunchtime is anything to go by, it's worth sampling. There's a fair selection of lagers on draught, and London Pride for bitter-drinking types.
/ Website: www.lock-tavern.co.uk Details: Mon-Thu 11am-midnight, Fri/ Sat 11am-1am, Sun 11am-11pm; no Amex. Food: Mon-Fri L till 3pm, D till 10pm, Sat L till 4pm, D till 9m, Sun L till 5pm, D till 9.30pm. DJ: Thu-Sun.

The Loft SW4

67 Clapham High St   7627 0792   10–2D

Offering more of a Manhattanite/West End vibe than you'd naturally expect in Clapham High Street, this large first-floor bar/restaurant has an impressive glass wall, running its full length. From the team behind Brixton's Plan B, but aiming for a more 'grown up' feel, it's quickly established itself as a major destination. / Website: www.theloft-clapham.co.uk Details: Mon-Thu 6pm-midnight, Fri 5.30pm-1.30pm, Sat noon-1.30pm, Sun noon-midnight. Food: same start times till 10pm during week, noon til 9pm Sat, 7pm Sun. DJ: Fri & Sat. Happy hour: Mon-Fri till 8pm, Sat & Sun till 7pm.

The Long Bar
Sanderson Hotel W1

50 Berners St   7300 5587   3–1D

It's no longer at the cutting edge of chic as once it was, but this descriptively-named bar – at a wacky design-hotel, just north of Oxford Street – can still be quite a 'scene'. If you're a sugar daddy with a bright young thing to impress, this may be just the place. / Website: www.sandersonlondon.com Details: Mon 11am-1am, Tue & Wed 11am-1.30am, Thu-Sat 11am-3am, Sun noon-10.30pm. Food: till midnight. DJ: Wed-Fri.

The Lonsdale W11

44-48 Lonsdale Rd   7727 4080   6–1B

Quietly located in a side street, this large and stylish three-floor spot remains a definitive Notting Hill bar. All human life is there... well at least all Notting Hill life. The cocktails are good too. / Website: www.thelonsdale.co.uk Details: Mon-Thu 6pm-midnight Fri & Sat 6pm-1am, Sun 6pm-11.30pm. Food: till 11pm. DJ: Fri-Sun.

Lost Society SW8

697 Wandsworth Rd   7652 6526   10–1C

Still remembered by some from its Tea Rooms des Artistes days, this intriguing 16th century barn – with its high ceilings and extravagant, chandeliered décor – has emerged as one of the hottest tickets in town. There is food – don't miss the '70s-homage 'Fondue Thursday'! – but the very extensive drinks and cocktails menu is the greater attraction. Cute small garden.
/ **Website:** www.lostsociety.co.uk **Details:** Sun-Wed 5pm-midnight, Thu 5pm-1am, Fri & Sat 5pm-2am. **Food:** till 11pm. **DJ:** Thu-Sat.

Lots Road Pub
& Dining Room SW10

114 Lots Rd   7352 6645   5–4B

Reproaching the eyesore that is Chelsea Harbour, this nice old Victorian pub building stands by the roundabout at the entrance to the complex. It was converted a few years ago into an airy modern hang-out, and it is rarely too crowded. An open kitchen offers a range of good but quite simple fare, at reasonable prices. / **Website:** www.lotsroadpub.co.uk **Details:** Mon-Sat Sun noon-10.30pm. **Food:** Mon-Sat till 9.30pm, Sun 10am-5pm.

Loungelover E1

1 Whitby St   7012 1234   1–2D

If you like Baz Luhrmann films ('Moulin Rouge', and so on), you'll love this. The owners of the fabulously OTT East End restaurant Les Trois Garçons brought similar 'maximalist' design values to this brilliant bar, awash with antiques, chandeliers and objets d'art. Even five years after it opened, it's still one of the coolest looking joints in town. / **Website:** www.loungelover.co.uk **Details:** Sun-Thu 6pm-midnight, Fri 5.30pm-1am, Sat 6pm-1am. **Food:** till 11pm. **DJ:** Fri & Sat.

Lowlander WC2

36 Drury Ln   7379 7446   4–1C

This stylish Covent Garden café/bar is a congenial spot, and especially useful pre-theatre. Dutch and Belgian beers are the main point – a dozen on draught from the shiny chrome pumps lined up along the bar (plus over 30 bottled varieties), making this one of London's better specialist beer halls. There is also a decent selection of wines. Everything is served Continental-style, by waiters. (There is now also a City outpost, at the junction of Mitre Street and Creechurch Lane.)
/ **Website:** www.lowlander.com **Details:** Tue-Sat 11.30am-11pm, Sun & Mon 11.30am-10.30pm. **Food:** till 11pm.

The Magdela Tavern NW3

2a South Hill Pk   7435 2503   8–1A

*It's the bullet holes still visible in the sides of the building, rather than the OK food and the updated interior, which win this pub by Hampstead Heath BR a place in all the guide books. This is the spot where cheated-on Ruth Ellis shot and killed her love rat, racing driver boyfriend… and subsequently became the last woman in England to be hanged, in 1955. / **Details:** Mon-Thu 11am-11pm, Fri & Sat 11am-12.30am, Sun noon-10.30pm; no Amex. **Food:** L till 2.30pm, D till 10pm, Sat all day, Sun noon-9.30pm.*

Mahiki W1

1 Dover St   7493 9529   3–3C

*If you've been living on Mars for the last few years, you'll have missed the fact that this 'Polynesian Paradise', just off Piccadilly, is a fave rave for younger royals. If you like dated kitsch, you'll love the bamboo walls, grass ceilings and wooden tiki figures here, where the action is spread over two floors – upstairs lounge, downstairs club. "Aloha!" indeed. / **Website:** www.mahiki.com **Details:** Mon-Fri 5.30pm-3.30am, Sat 7.30pm-3.30am. **Food:** till midnight. **DJ:** Mon-Sat. **Cover charge may apply.***

Malmaison EC1

18-21 Charterhouse St   7012 3700   9–1B

*The look of this Farringdon design-hotel is a little bit Identikit-trendy, but its bar – which overlooks a bustling brasserie, and which offers a selection of deep sofas – makes a civilised place for a drink. You can choose a (classic) cocktail from the list, but wine and unmixed spirits are equally popular. / **Website:** www.malmaison.com **Details:** Mon-Sat 11am-midnight, Sun noon-midnight. **Food:** till 11pm.*

Mandarin Bar
Mandarin Oriental Hyde Pk Hotel SW1

66 Knightsbridge   7235 2000   5–1D

*After the imposing late-Victorian façade and the elegantly marbled lobby – the building was originally constructed as gentlemen's apartments – it's a surprise to come across the 'happening' cocktail bar of this grand Knightsbridge hotel. It's a sleek-looking destination, and is perhaps over-popular at peak times. / **Website:** www.mandarinoriental.com **Details:** Mon-Sat 11am-2am, Sun 11am-midnight. **Food:** always available.*

The Marquess Tavern N1

32 Canonbury St 7354 2975 8–2D

Charmingly situated in a pretty residential quarter of leafy Canonbury, this imposing mid-19th-century Young's hostelry was successfully relaunched a couple of years ago. There's been a subsequent change of ownership, but the plain-vanilla gastropub format – and the personnel – were largely unaffected. / **Website:** www.themarquesstavern.co.uk **Details:** Mon-Wed 5pm-11pm, Thu noon-11pm, Fri & Sat noon-midnight, Sun noon-10.30pm. **Food:** till 10pm.

Mason's Arms SW8

169 Battersea Park Rd 7622 2007 10–1C

This light and bright gastropub, grottily located next to Battersea Park BR, was one of the front-runners in the transformation of London's pub-scene in the mid-'90s. It's always offered pretty good food, and has proved itself to be quite a 'stayer'. / **Website:** www.fullers.co.uk **Details:** noon-11pm. **Food:** Mon-Fri noon-3pm, 6pm-10pm, Sat noon-4pm, 6-10pm, Sun noon-4pm, 6-9pm.

Matchbar

37-38 Margaret St W1 7499 3443 3–1C
45-47 Clerkenwell Rd EC1 7250 4002 9–1C

This lounge bar duo epitomise the smooth, understated contemporary look that swept across London in the late '90s. What they do is no longer remarkable – but they achieve it with a consistency and style that still sets them apart from many rivals (not least when it comes to mixing a decent cocktail). / **Website:** www.matchbar.com.

The Mayflower SE16

117 Rotherhithe St 7237 4088 11–1A

An historic Rotherhithe pub, near the departure point of the Pilgrim Fathers for the New World. Its terrace, overhanging the river, affords a wonderful view over the Thames – one of the reasons it attracts a fair mix of customers. / **Website:** www.themayflowerpub.co.uk **Details:** Mon-Thu 11am-3pm, 5.15pm-11pm, Sat & Sun 11am-11pm (summer 11am-11pm); no Amex. **Food:** Mon-Fri L till 2.30pm, D 6pm-9.30pm, Sat noon-9.30pm.

Medcalf EC1

40 Exmouth Mkt   7833 3533   9–1A

Located on Clerkenwell's 'Little Trendy Street', this understated diner-by-day-bar-by-night is situated in an old butcher's shop and features regularly-changing art displays. Continental beers are the most common drink, but wine is also popular, and there's also quite a range of cocktails.
/ **Website:** www.medcalfbar.co.uk **Details:** Mon-Thu & Sat noon-11pm, Fri noon-1am, Sun noon-6pm; no Amex. **Food:** till 9.45pm, Thu-Sat till 10.15pm.

Met Bar
Metropolitan Hotel W1

18-19 Old Park Ln   7447 5865   3–4A

At the foot of what is still Park Lane's only really trendy hotel (and below the famous Nobu restaurant), this once-crazily-fashionable bar is by no means as cutting-edge as in times gone by. However, mortals – ie non-hotel-residents, non-members – are still permitted to enter only till 9pm.
/ **Website:** www.metbar.co.uk **Details:** . **Food:** till 9pm (non-guests), till 1am (members and hotel residents). **DJ:** Tue-Sat.

Milk & Honey W1

Poland St   07000 MLKHNY   3–2D

One of the few bars with outlets in both NYC and London, this speakeasy-style Soho operation – inspired by the spirit of '40s American jazz, apparently – is renowned as one of the cooler destinations in town. At the request of the management, we've not put the full address, as non-members are required (and welcome) to book ahead. / **Website:** www.mlkhny.com
Details: Mon-Fri 6pm-3am, Sat 7pm-3am, closed Sun . **Food:** till 11pm (members 2am).

Mint Leaf SW1

1 Suffolk Pl   7930 9020   2–2C

Sneak round the back of an imposing bank building at the near end of Pall Mall, and you'll find the stairs to this impressive, darkly-decorated bar/restaurant (designed by the same man who did the celebrated Hakkasan). Cocktails (or Indian beers) are the tipples of choice, and you can move on to some sophisticated (and pricey) 'nouvelle Indian' food in the adjoining restaurant. / **Website:** www.mintleafrestaurant.com **Details:** Mon-Wed noon-midnight, Thu & Fri noon-1am, Sat 5.30pm-1am, Sun 5.30pm-midnight. **Food:** till 11pm. **DJ:** Fri & Sat. **Live music:** weekends.

Mint Leaf Lounge EC2

Angel Ct   7600 0992   9–2C

In a dreary alley near the Bank of England, this beautiful, shimmering new bar/restaurant (nothing like the dark West End original) would have seemed unthinkable a few years ago. It's best to go easy on the seriously expensive nouvelle Indian bar snacks – there's also a restaurant – but the luxurious bar, with its white leather banquettes, is one of the plushest City watering holes. / **Website:** www.mintleaflounge.com **Details:** Mon-Wed noon-midnight, Thu-Fri noon-1am. **Food:** Mon-Fri L till 3pm, D 5.30pm-11pm.

Momo W1

25 Heddon St   7434 4040   3–2C

When Mourad Mazouz – who is also the man behind fashionista's favourite restaurant Sketch – opened this Moroccan-styled den it was the talk of the town, with early sightings of Tom Cruise with then-wife Nicole Kidman. Those heady days may be long gone, but the party hasn't slowed down much – either in the basement Kemia bar or in the hugely atmospheric restaurant above. Members only after 11pm. / **Website:** www.momoresto.com **Details:** noon-midnight (bar noon-3am). **Food:** Mon-Sat L noon-2.30pm, D 6.30pm-11.30pm, D Sun 6.30pm-11pm. **DJ:** Wed-Sat. **Live music:** Tue.

Monkey Chews NW5

2 Queens Cr   7482 4981   8–2B

It's hard to pigeon-hole this drinking den – a converted corner pub – in a quiet backstreet north of Chalk Farm tube. It does food, but it's not a typical gastropub; it has regular DJs and live music, but isn't really a DJ bar; it does a good line in cocktails, but isn't really a cocktail bar. According to the website it's "the kind of bar Tom Waits sings about". Now you know. / **Website:** www.monkeychews.com **Details:** Mon-Fri 5pm-11pm, Sat & Sun noon-11pm. **Food:** Mon-Sat 7pm-11pm, Sun noon-10pm. **DJ:** Fri & Sat. **Live music:** Tue-Thu.

Montgomery Place W11

31 Kensington Park Rd   7792 3921   6–1A

This sensual, cosy and elegantly low-lit bar is a serious cocktail lounge of a quality you don't come across that often. It's a smooth destination in its own right, or – if you can drag yourself away – offers a terrific warm up for a night in Notting Hill. / **Website:** www.montgomeryplace.co.uk **Details:** 5pm-midnight. **Food:** till 11.30pm.

The Morgan Arms E3

43 Morgan St   8980 6389   1–2D

One of the better operations in the (rather up-and-down) Geronimo Inns gastropub group, this buzzing Bow boozer is a relatively upmarket sort of place, in a style which is still relatively rare in the East End. / Website: www.geronimo-inns.co.uk
Details: *Sun-Thu noon-11pm, Fri & Sat noon-midnight; no Amex.*
Food: *Mon-Sat L noon-3pm, D 7pm-10pm, Sun L noon-4pm, D 6pm-9pm.*

Motcomb's SW1

26 Motcomb St   7235 6382   5–1D

A long-established, clubby and art-filled Belgravia wine bar, whose regulars give the appearance of having been in attendance for decades. In the middle of the day, lunchers take up much of the space. / Website: www.motcombs.co.uk
Details: *Mon-Sat noon-11pm, Sun noon-6pm.* **Food:** *L till 6pm, D 6.30pm-11pmpm.* **Cover charge may apply.**

Mother Bar EC1

333 Old St   7739 5949   9–1D

Not a place for quiet contemplation, perhaps, but this dark space sits over Shoreditch's well-known music venue 333 and offers the chance for a breather, relatively speaking, from the frenetic scene down below (with DJs nightly). Quieter early-evening, it revs up as the night goes on, and is open long into the wee hours. / Website: www.333mother.com **Details:** *Mon-Wed 8pm-3am, Thu-Sun 8pm-4am ; no Amex.* **DJ:** *nightly.* **Live music:** *most nights.* **Cover charge may apply.**

The Museum Tavern WC1

49 Gt Russel St   7242 8987   4–1B

The museum in question is the British, and a location bang opposite the entrance guarantees a pretty touristy crowd here. Not that this isn't a fine Victorian pub – many of the fittings are original and there are some very nice etched glass and mirrors. It's also quite a place if you are into real ale – they have seven on tap, guest beers and two festivals a year. / Food: till 10.30pm.

Na Zdrowie WC1

11 Little Turnstile   7831 9679   2–1D

Just behind Holborn tube, in a tiny alley, this small and funky Polish bar is very popular. If offers over 60 different types of vodka – from Luksusowa (potato) to Wyborowa (pineapple), via Ajacoco (coconut) – as well as four Polish bottled beers, so it's almost certain that you can find a tipple to suit you. / Details: Mon 4pm-11pm, Tue-Wed, 12.30am-11pm, Fri 12.30pm-11.30pm, Sat 6pm-11pm, closed Sun; no Amex. Food: till 10pm.

The Nag's Head SW1

53 Kinnerton St   7235 1135   5–1D

A top central choice for a quiet pint. Dating from 1777, this tiny Belgravia freehouse is as rambling and cosy a spot as you might hope to find, and it has an excellent 'villagey' location in a back lane, only five minutes walk from Hyde Park Corner… if you know the way. Hurrah! – no mobiles. / **Food:** *till 9.30pm.*

The Narrow E14

44 Narrow St   7592 7950   11–1B

A nice East End riverside pub, recently modernised, with a large waterside terrace, impressive views and a good-quality contemporary dining room. All the hype surrounding its proprietor Gordon Ramsay, however, might lead you to expect something more… / **Website:** www.gordonramsay.com
Details: *noon-1am.* **Food:** *L till 3pm, D till 10pm.*

19:20 EC1

19-20 Great Sutton St   7253 1920   9–1B

From the mosaic water feature in the window to the colourful pool tables inside, this Clerkenwell bar – former watchmakers' premises – is a young designer's dream. There are bars both on the ground floor and in the basement – connected by a sweeping circular staircase – where a post-work crowd gathers to quaff inventive cocktails, or Beamish and Kronenbourg on tap. / **Website:** www.19-20.co.uk **Details:** *Mon-Fri noon-11pm, Sat 7pm-1.30am, closed Sun.* **Food:** *noon-3pm, 6pm-10pm.* **DJ:** *Thu & Fri.*

93 Feet East E1

150 Brick Ln   7247 3293   9–1D

You don't have to be going to a gig in the warehouse-y main hall to make a visit to this large East End venue worthwhile. You can just chill out in the loungy, less sparse 'Pink Bar' (which also has regular DJs and dancing), or the good-looking outside courtyard, where there's often a barbecue.
/ **Website:** www.93feeteast.co.uk **Details:** *Mon-Thu 5pm-11pm, Fri 5pm-1am, Sat 5pm-1am, Sun 11am-10.30pm.* **Food:** *BBQ 5pm-late (Sat & Sun 2pm till late).* **DJ:** *most nights (check website for details).* **Live music:** *Mon-Fri (check website for details).*

No.5
Cavendish Square W1

5 Cavendish Sq   7079 5000   3–1C

Imagine a Moscow oligarch's palace, and you may get something of the feeling of this wonderfully OTT townhouse, just north of Oxford Street. There's a restaurant (on the first floor), and you can even stay the night in decadent splendour, but the ground-floor bar is a great attraction in its own right (assuming, of course, you like a WAG-y crowd). Big cover charge after 11pm (Fri & Sat). / **Website:** www.no5ltd.com
Details: Mon-Thu 10am-1am, Fri 10am-3am, Sat 6pm-3am, closed Sun.
Food: canâpés served in bar all day. **DJ:** Fri & Sat. **Cover charge may apply.**

Nordic W1

25 Newman St   7631 3174   3–1D

Nordic tourism brochures by the entrance add authenticity to this cool Scandinavian venture, in the shadow of the Telecom Tower, where the neutral décor is enhanced by glimpses of weird Scandiness. From Red Eric lager to an impressive array of bottled lagers, cocktails and vodkas, there's an intriguing range of Nordic tipples, plus a selection of meatballs, herrings, gravadlax and so on to help soften their after-effects.
/ **Website:** www.nordicbar.com **Details:** Mon-Thu noon-11pm,
Fri noon-midnight, Sat 6pm-midnight, closed Sun. **Food:** L till 3pm, D till 10pm.
Happy hour: Mon-Fri 5.30pm-8pm.

The Norfolk Arms WC1

28 Leigh St   7388 3937   8–4C

"Is it a tapas bar? Is it a gastropub? Who cares? It's a great place!" – one of the comments we received in our most recent restaurant survey on this revamped Bloomsbury boozer. There's a good range of drinks on offer too – the Spanish-heavy wine list you would expect, but also a fair selection of beers and cocktails. / **Website:** www.norfolkarms.co.uk **Details:** Mon-Sat 11am-11pm, Sun 11am-10.30pm. **Food:** Mon-Sat L noon-3pm,
D 6.30pm-10.15pm, Sun noon-10.15pm.

Northbank EC4

1 Paul's Walk   7329 9299   9–3B

"New York cocktails to Cornish ales" – that's the range of drinking possibilities on offer at this City bar (and British restaurant). Its most obvious virtues, though, are its extensive terraces, and its views of Tate Modern, and the 'wobbly bridge'.
/ **Website:** www.northbankrestaurant.com **Details:** Mon-Sat noon-11pm,
Sun noon-5pm.

The Notting Hill Arts Club W11

21 Notting Hill Gate   7460 4459   6–2B

Always busy, this slightly grungy/studenty basement bar and club is a great place to go for a boogie and a drink in relaxed and intimate surroundings. It specialises in a music programme of DJs and bands (as well as art shows), and there is a dance floor adjoining the bar. / **Website:** www.nottinghillartsclub.com
Details: Tue-Fri 4pm-2am, Sat 4pm-2am, Sun 4pm-1am, closed Mon; no Amex. **Food:** L&D. **DJ & Live music:** nightly. **Happy hour:** Mon-Sat 6pm-9.30pm.

O-Bar W1

83-85 Wardour St   7437 3490   3–2D

Prominently located on a central Soho corner, this three-level operation is decked out with a plush Gothic theme, and is usually heaving with a mixed crowd of twentysomething (21+) lads and ladettes on the pull. / **Website:** www.the-obar.co.uk
Details: Mon-Thu 5pm-3am, Fri 4pm-3am, Sat 3pm-3am, Sun 4pm-10.30pm; no Amex. **Food:** till midnight, Fri & Sat till 2am. **DJ:** nightly. **Happy hour:** Mon-Sun 4pm-8pm.

The Old Bull & Bush NW3

North End Rd   8905 5456   8–1A

"Come, come, come and make eyes at me, Down at the old Bull and Bush", ran the catchy '20s hit song. Modern-day romantics – eyes hopefully sparkling after a bracing walk on nearby Hampstead Heath – may be equally impressed with this upmarket, spacious pub with its low ceilings, exposed beams and deep leather sofas. / **Website:** www.thebullandbush.co.uk
Details: noon-11pm. **Food:** till 9.30pm.

The Old Coffee House W1

49 Beak St   7437 2197   3–2D

This traditional corner boozer is one of the very nicest pubs around Soho – just thoroughly cosy and unpretentious, it offers a good range of beers and lagers and attracts a wide-ranging crowd. The name is, of course, completely misleading nowadays – all is explained in a notice by the door. / **Details:** 11am-11pm; no Amex. **Food:** Mon-Sat L till 3pm.

The Old Dr Butler's Head EC2

Masons Ave   7606 3504   9–2C

This City pub, in an alley off Moorgate, is owned by quality brewer Shepherd Neame. Though the place is known for its historical associations (a 17th-century quack who marketed a brand of medicinal ale), it doesn't feel markedly more ancient than many comparable establishments.
/ Website: www.shepherd-neame.co.uk Details: closed Sat & Sun. Food: till 3pm.

The Old School Yard SE1

111 Long Ln   7357 6281   9–4C

School days provide the theme for this 'bar & playground', tucked-away five minutes' walk south of Guy's Hospital, where help in reverting to childhood is provided by a long list of cocktails presented comic book-style. Fashionistas should probably head on elsewhere, but if you're in the mood for a rollicking good time, this might be the place.
/ Website: www.theoldschoolyard.com Details: Tue-Thu 5.30pm-11pm, Fri & Sat 5.30pm-12.30am, Sun 5.30pm-10.30pm. DJ & Live music: occasionally. Happy hour: 5.30pm-8pm, all night Sun.

The Old Ship W6

25 Upper Mall   8748 2593   7–2B

Despite being on the site of one of the oldest inns in Hammersmith, this nautically-themed pub, overlooking the river, doesn't feel nearly as historic as The Dove (five minutes' walk away). It certainly doesn't want for custom, though. On summer weekends, when its large terrace and neighbouring grass area come into their own, the place heaves with a twentysomething crowd which seems to include every Aussie and Kiwi in town. / Website: www.oldshipw6.co.uk Details: Mon-Fri 8am-11pm, Sat 8am-midnight, Sun 8am-10.30pm. Food: Mon-Sat till 10.30pm, Sun till10pm.

Ye Olde Cheshire Cheese EC4

145 Fleet St   7353 6170   9–2A

In Baedeker's 1904 guide, this incredibly historic-feeling City pub (1667) – the local in its time of Dickens and Dr Johnson – was already a recommended London attraction. Since then, little has changed and, especially in winter when the real coal fire is burning, its warren of bars offers one of the best tastes of olde England in town. It attracts a good local following, as well as tourists. / Details: Mon-Sat 11am-11pm, Sun noon-5pm . Food: noon-9.30pm.

Ye Olde Mitre Tavern EC1

I Ely Court   7405 4751   9–2A

When you finally locate this very ancient (1546) wooden tavern (down a tiny, dank alley off Hatton Garden), it feels like you've stepped back in time – especially in winter, when the outside drinking area is very quiet. There are a couple of connected rooms – the snug panelled front bar, and a cosy back one – in which to enjoy a fair range of ales and lagers. / **Details:** *closed Sat & Sun.* **Food:** *till 9.15pm.*

Ye Olde White Bear NW3

Well Rd, New End   7435 3758   8–1A

Even the lamp post outside this ancient inn, in a pretty part of Hampstead, is on a tilt. There's an open fire, too, making this one of the more attractive destinations in what is arguably London's premier historic village. It's an ideal place for a reviver after a walk on the Heath, and its offer includes a reasonable range of real ales. / **Details:** *Mon-Wed noon-11pm, Thu-Sat noon-11.30pm, sat 1130-1130. Sun noon-11pm.* **Food:** *till 9pm.*

The Lobby Bar
One Aldwych WC2

I Aldwych   7300 1070   2–2D

As a place to drink, this stylish design-hotel, on the edge of Covent Garden, seems to have faded in popularity a little in recent times. The double-height entrance lobby, however – which is largely given over to the cocktail bar – remains an elegant space in which to enjoy a drink at any time of day. / **Website:** www.onealdwych.com **Details:** *Mon-Sat 8am-midnight, Sun 8am-10.30pm.* **Food:** *B 8am-11am, L noon-5pm, bar snacks 5.50pm-midnight.* **DJ:** *Sat 8pm-11.30pm.*

Opal
L'Etranger SW7

36 Gloucester Rd   7584 1118   5–1B

An upmarket bar, located beneath a French-Oriental restaurant of some ambition (or, a cynic would say, some pretension). Until 10pm, it's a loungey sort of place, where the emphasis is very much on enjoying the range of exotic cocktails and snacks to match. After that time, the DJs spin, and the atmosphere becomes clubbier (in the South Kensington sense). / **Website:** www.opalbar.co.uk **Details:** *Wed-Sat 9pm-2am, closed Sun-Tue.* **Food:** *till 11pm.* **DJ:** *nightly.* **Cover charge may apply.**

Oriel SW1

50-51 Sloane Sq   7730 2804   5–2D

*In spirit and appearance – if decidedly not in culinary
achievement – this prominently-located bar/brasserie, on a
corner of Sloane Square, is perhaps London's closest match
to its Parisian equivalents. It's busy around the clock and –
especially if you can get an outside table – makes a great place
to watch the world go by. Alternatively, there's a downstairs
wine bar which is a particular haunt of after-work drinkers.*
/ **Details:** *Mon-Sat 8.30am-10.45pm, Sun 9am-10.30pm.* **Food:** *till
10.45pm.*

Oscar Bar
Charlotte St Hotel W1

15-17 Charlotte St   7806 2000   2–1C

*More of an attraction than the adjoining restaurant,
this spacious and elegant bar – part of a Fitzrovia boutique
hotel – comes into its own on sunny days, when the whole
of the front opens up to the street.*
/ **Website:** *www.charlottestreethotel.com* **Details:** *Mon-Sat 11am-11pm,
Sun 11am-8pm.* **Food:** *restaurant 11pm, bar all day till 10.30pm.*

Oxo Tower SE1

Barge House St   7803 3888   9–3A

*Location, location and, er, location – those are the attractions
of the bar at this famous bar/brasserie/restaurant. Located
on the seventh floor of the landmark South Bank complex,
it enjoys splendid views over the river, and of the other side
of the Thames. There are two dining options – a brasserie
as well as a swanky restaurant – but both are very expensive
for what they are.* / **Website:** *www.harveynichols.com* **Details:** *Mon-Wed
11am-11pm, Thu-Sat 11am-11.30pm, Sun noon-10.30pm.* **Food:** *till
10.30pm.*

The Palmerston SE22

91 Lordship Ln   8693 1629   1–4D

*A chef from one of the capital's longest-running restaurant
success-stories (Bibendum) has helped make this East Dulwich
boozer quite a south London star. Much of the panelled interior
is now given over to the dining room, which has benefitted
greatly from not being too tarted up.*
/ **Website:** *www.thepalmerston.net* **Details:** *noon-11pm.* **Food:** *till 10pm.*

The Pantechnicon Rooms SW1

10 Motcomb St   7730 6074   5–1D

The team from the Thomas Cubitt (see also) deserve a prize for making Belgravia more habitable, thanks to their brand of plush boozers, of which this is the second example. Both are upmarket but quite affordable places of a type that are otherwise totally lacking nearby. Every sort of alcohol (including premium champagnes) is on offer, as well as small bites to full meals (in the grand upstairs room).
/ **Website:** www.thepantechnicon.com **Details:** Mon-Fri noon-11pm, Sat & Sun 8.30am-11pm. **Food:** Mon-Fri noon-10pm, Sat & Sun 8.30am-10pm.

Paradise by Way of Kensal Green W10

19 Kilburn Ln   8969 0098   1–2B

Despite a recent change of ownership and a major revamp, this long-running Kensal Green success story just goes on and on, packing in hip media folk from far and wide (particularly nearby Notting Hill). It's a huge, rambling place, with a large bar, a great roof terrace, an upstairs dance floor and a very attractive dining room. / **Website:** www.theparadise.co.uk
Details: Mon-Wed noon-midnight, Thu noon-1am, Fri & Sat noon-2am, Sun noon-11.30pm; no Amex. **Food:** till 10.50pm. **DJ:** Fri & Sat.
Live music: varies.

Parker McMillan EC1

47 Chiswell St   7256 5883   9–1C

In a rambling series of atmospheric brick vaults (once part of the old Whitbread Brewery, opposite), this relaxed bar is one of the few decent hang-outs near the Barbican. An ever-changing programme of live music and open-mic nights provide much of the attraction. For the summer, there is also a small terrace. / **Website:** www.parkermcmillan.co.uk **Details:** Tue-Fri 4pm-2am, closed Sat-Mon. **Food:** always available. **DJ:** varies - see website.
Live music: varies-see website. **Happy hour:** all night Tue & Wed, 5pm-8pm Thu & Fri.

The Peasant EC1

240 St John St   7336 7726   9–1A

This corner pub in Clerkenwell — featuring a large, traditional horseshoe bar and a selection of circus-themed artwork — was one of the first places, back in the '90s, to be sympathetically-converted into what we now think of as a classic gastropub. A fair array of beers and ciders (including 30 by the bottle) is available. Eat tapas-style at the bar, or in the restaurant upstairs. / **Website:** www.thepeasant.co.uk
Details: noon-11pm. **Food:** D only Tue-Sat 6pm-10.30pm.

La Perla WC2

28 Maiden Ln   7240 7400   4–3D

It's not the last word in sophistication, but – for a fun night out that won't break the bank – there are far worse places than this Latino cantina, which is packed on busy nights with a raucous, largely twentysomething crowd. Margaritas, tequilas, and rums are the order of the day, and there's some cheap (and not bad) Tex/Mex scoff to help soak 'em up.
/ **Website:** www.cafepacifico-laperla.com **Details:** Mon-Sat noon-11pm, Sun 1pm-10.30pm. **Food:** till 10.50pm. **Happy hour:** 4pm-7pm.

The Pig's Ear SW3

35 Old Church St   7352 2908   5–3C

This prettily-sited Chelsea corner boozer traded for many years as the 'Front Page', but a while ago was relaunched – oddly, but successfully – as a Belle Epoque brasserie-style operation. There's now a proper restaurant upstairs, but the bar remains a convivial place if you just want a glass of wine, or a pint.
/ **Details:** Mon-Sat noon-11pm, Sun noon-10.30pm. **Food:** Mon-Fri 12.30-3pm, Sat 12.30pm-3.30pm Sun 12.30pm-4pm.

Pilot W4

56 Wellesley Rd   8994 0828   7–2A

There aren't many places to drink or eat in the area south of Gunnersbury Tube, and this handy gastropub fills both needs. It's part of a small chain (which includes the Mason's Arms and Stonemasons') and adopts the same casual and relaxing style. In summer, the outside area at the back comes into its own.
/ **Details:** Mon-Sat noon-11pm, Sun noon-10.30pm. **Food:** L till 3pm, D till 10pm.

Plan B SW9

418 Brixton Rd   7733 0926   10–2D

*They don't ever seem to have needed a plan B at this Brixton bar, which was THE DJ bar of the moment when in opened in 2002. Nowadays it's perhaps in a less edgy groove, but a wide mix of fans still travel from far and wide, especially for its well-known Fri and Sat nights (not to mention its early evening 2-for-1 happy hour). / **Website:** www.plan-brixton.co.uk*
Details: Mon-Thu 7pm-3am, Fri & Sat 8pm-5am; no Amex. **DJ:** Fri-Sun. **Live music:** occasionally. **Happy hour:** till 11pm. **Cover charge may apply.**

The Player W1

8-12 Broadwick St   7494 9125   3–2D

If you didn't know it was there, you'd pass by this inconspicuous door in a sleazy part of Soho without ever thinking of going downstairs to one of the best-reputed cocktail bars in town. Its plush banquettes make ideal lounging-points, typically for execs who fancy themselves as Players in the music biz. This was once a members' bar, but now it's open to all – an invitation it would be rude not to take up. / **Website:** *www.thplyr.com* **Details:** *Mon-Wed 5.30pm-midnight, Thu 5.30pm-1am, Fri 5.30pm-2am, Sat 7pm-2am.* **Food:** *till late.* **DJ:** *Thu-Sat.* **Cover charge may apply.**

Plumbers Arms SW1

14 Lower Belgrave St   7730 4067   2–4B

Students of modern history will not wish to miss out on a visit to this Georgian boozer, off Eaton Square, famously the pub where, in 1974, Lady Lucan announced her husband's failed attempt to kill her (though he had, by mistake, killed the family nanny). That's as aristocratic as the place's associations get, however, and it's really a pretty typical 'local' nowadays. / **Details:** *Mon-Thu 11am-11pm, Fri 11am-11.30pm.* **Food:** *till 10pm, Fri till 2.30pm.*

Polo Bar
Westbury Hotel W1

New Bond St   7629 7755   3–2C

Like the Westbury Hotel of which it's part, there's nothing particularly distinctive or glamorous about this comfy bar, but it exudes a certain plush, polished charm, aided by its retinue of discreet, professional staff. For a posh cocktail in the heart of Mayfair, you could do very much worse. / **Website:** *www.westburymayfair.com* **Details:** *11am-1am.* **Food:** *till 12.30am.*

Portobello Gold W11

95 Portobello Rd   7460 4900   6–2B

Despite its position in the heart of Notting Hill, and despite having been one of the first pubs in town to be given the bar-treatment, this gentrified boozer has never attracted the more self-conscious end of the local trendy crowd. Market traders rub shoulders with tourists (even President Bill Clinton woz here) in the bar and large dining conservatory, and there's quite an interesting list of drinks. / **Website:** *www.portobellogold.com* **Details:** *Mon-Thu 10am-midnight, Fri & Sat 10am-12.30am, Sun 10am-11.30pm.* **Food:** *till 11.15pm.* **Happy hour:** *5pm-7pm.* **Cover charge may apply.**

Potemkin EC1

144 Clerkenwell Rd   7278 6661   9–1A

There's nothing particularly Russian about the décor at this bright, minimalist bar, which is named after the soldier-lover of Czarina Catherine II. The drinks selection, though, could have done even Boris Yeltsin proud – a bewildering array of vodkas, cocktails, beers and spirits. In the basement there's a restaurant, but the bar itself offers a good range of zakuski (snacks) – from pickles and soups to caviar.
/ Website: www.potemkin.co.uk Details: Mon-Fri noon-11pm, Sat 6pm-11pm, closed Sun. Food: L till 3pm, Sat D 6-11pm.

The Prince Arthur E8

95 Forest Rd   7249 9996   1–1D

This London Fields boozer has recently been revamped – in trademark understated period style – by Tom and Ed Martin. As cognoscenti of London boozers will know, the brothers – most famous for the Gun, near Canary Wharf – specialise in good-quality but pricey gastropubs, and this one is no exception. / Website: www.theprincearthurlondonfields.com
Details: Mon-Thu 4pm-11pm, Fri noon-11pm, Sat & Sun 10.30am-11pm; no Amex. Food: till 10pm.

The Prince Bonaparte W2

80 Chepstow Rd   7313 9491   6–1B

It used to be at the basic end of trendy gastropubs – drawing a slightly less posey Notting Hillbilly set as a result – but this large and attractive Bayswater boozer has been cosied up a bit in recent years (and further refurbished by its new, late-2008 owners). Food remains a big part of its offer, and this is still a very popular local. No children. / Details: Mon-Sat noon-11pm, Sun noon-9.30pm. Food: Mon-Fri noon-3.30pm, 6pm-10.30pm, Sat & Sun noon-4.30m, 6pm-10.30pm.

The Prince Of Wales SW11

186 Battersea Bridge Rd   7228 0395   10–1C

A good all-purpose spot, down Battersea way, this inviting boozer (formerly known as the Settle Inn) makes a welcoming winter destination, and has an attractive beer garden for the summer. It's a friendly place too, and they make quite an effort on the food front. / Website: www.theprinceofwalesbattersea.co.uk
Details: Mon-Sat noon-11pm, Sun noon-10.30pm. Food: till 10pm.

Princess Victoria SW12

217 Uxbridge Rd   8749 5886   7–1B

A newly-revamped pub, on a lonely bit of Shepherd's Bush highway, that's already winning awards, thanks to the magnificent restoration of its huge Victorian building, its very superior wine list and its good selection of ales. Other attractions include quality cooking, and even an outdoor 'artisan' food market on Sat mornings.
/ **Website:** www.princessvictoria.co.uk

Priory House W14

58 Milson Rd   7371 3999   7–1D

In the warren of backstreets behind Olmypia, this dim-lit bar makes a surprising find. It's well worth discovering, for its unpretentious yet stylish atmosphere, quality cocktails and wines, plus – if required – yummy tapas. For maximum cosiness, try to bag one of the dark leather booths (though these seem to be held back for diners).
/ **Website:** www.housebars.co.uk/prioryhouse **Details:** Mon-Fri noon-11.30pm, Sat 5pm-11.30pm, closed Sun; no Amex. **Food:** Mon-Fri noon-3pm, Sat 5pm-11pm.

Prism EC3

147 Leadenhall St   7256 3888   9–2D

This low-ceilinged bar is hidden away in the bowels of Harvey Nichols' City restaurant outpost, and couldn't be in starker contrast to the cavernous dining room above in a former banking hall. Comfortable cream leather banquettes add to the character of the chic dark-wood décor. Towards the weekend, look out for occasional DJs (and even circus acts!).
/ **Website:** www.harveynichols.com **Details:** Mon-Fri 11am-11pm, closed Sat & Sun. **Food:** always available. **DJ:** Fri.

The Prospect of Whitby E1

57 Wapping Wall   7481 1095   11–1A

Built in 1520, this famous Wapping hostelry is – as proudly proclaimed over the door – the oldest of London's riverside taverns. Past customers include Henry VIII, Pepys, Dickens, Turner and Captain Cook. Although the décor has changed over the years, the place retains many wonderful period features including flagged floors, a lovely pewter bar and pillars made from ships' masts. All this, and a pleasant Thames-side terrace.
/ **Food:** till 9.30pm.

The Punch & Judy WC2

40 The Mkt   7379 0923   4–3D

*Few self-respecting Londoners would admit to being regulars of this expensive tourist-trap pub – located in the eaves of Covent Garden's covered market. Pop in at a quiet time, though, and the view from the terrace of the "Actors' Church" – or, as many people think of it, the one in 'My Fair Lady' – is impressive. / **Details:** Mon-Sat 10am-11pm, Sun noon-10.30pm. **Food:** Mon-Thu, Sun till 9pm, Fri till 8pm, Sat till 7pm.*

The Punch Tavern EC4

99 Fleet St   7353 6658   9–2A

*This City-fringe pub is grander than your average boozer (appropriately for a part of the building where the celebrated magazine was conceived in 1841). It's taken on almost a coffee house vibe in recent years, with the launch of 'Club Mangia' – there's a buffet option for eating, plus coffee and cakes. It offers a good marriage of old and new, and traditionalists still have the attraction of a display of Punch and Judy memorabilia. / **Website:** www.punchtavern.com **Details:** Mon-Wed 7am-11pm, Thu & Fri 7am-midnight, Sat 10am-5pm. **Food:** buffet till 3pm, full menu 11am-11pm.*

Purple
Sanderson Hotel W1

50 Berners St   7300 9500   3–1D

*The inner sanctum of Ian Schrager's poseurs' paradise design-hotel, just north of Oxford Street. It's a superior choice to the better-known Long Bar, but more difficult to enter – if you're not a resident (or "on the list"), you're unlikely to be coming in. / **Website:** www.morganshotelgroup.com **Details:** Mon-Sat 6pm-3am, Sun 6pm-midnight.*

Quaglino's SW1

16 Bury St   7930 6767   3–3D

*How glamorous it seemed when this vast venture opened, back in 1993. These days, it doesn't draw the 'A'-list as once it did (or even the 'B'- or 'C'- list). Still the comfortable bar – which to an extent overlooks the diners below – still makes quite a striking venue, and is still pretty popular with St James's locals. No children in bar. / **Website:** www.quaglinos.co.uk **Details:** Mon-Thu 11.30am-1.30am, Fri & Sat 5.30pm-3.30am, Sun noon-midnight. **Food:** till 11.30pm.*

Queen's Arms SW1

11 Warwick Way   7834 3313   2–4B

Now part of a group which rejoices in the name 'Food & Fuel',
this corner boozer — formerly called 'The Page in Pimlico' —
has recently been relaunched as a good and friendly, straight-
down-the-line gastropub. In an area that's remarkably thin for
quality eating and drinking, it has deservedly found a ready
*following. / **Details:** noon-11pm. **Food:** till 10pm.*

Queen's Head W6

Brook Gn   7603 3174   7–1C

With a few tweaks, this wonderful, rambling old tavern
on Brook Green could be one of the most atmospheric pubs
in town. As it is, it still makes a cosy place in winter, and in
summer there is the added attraction of a vast, and very well-
maintained beer garden — one of the best in west London.
There's a huge menu, ranging from quite good snacks to over-
*pricey main dishes. / **Website:** www.thespiritgroup.com **Details:** Mon-Sat*
*11am-11pm, Sun noon-10.30pm. **Food:** till 10pm, Sun till 9pm.*

Queen's Head
& Artichoke NW1

30-32 Albany St   7916 6206   8–4B

This attractively revamped Victorian tavern, near Euston's Little
India, is popular both with locals and with medics from the
nearby Royal College of Physicians. It's fine just drinking in the
laid back downstairs bar, but there's some very decent tapas
if you're hungry (and heartier nosh in the dining room above).
*/ **Website:** www.theartichoke.net **Details:** 11am-11pm. **Food:** L noon-3pm,*
D 6-10.15pm, Sun till 10pm.

The Rake SE1

14 Winchester Walk   7407 0557   9–4C

Beer-lover heaven is to be found at this tiny pub, run by
Utobeer (the beer specialists with a stand in Borough Market,
opposite). The interior is no great shakes — best to visit on a
sunny day when you can sit outside and sample one of their
*120 specialist brews. / **Website:** www.utobeer.co.uk **Details:** Mon-Fri*
*noon-11pm, Sat 10am-11pm, closed Sun. **Food:** sandwiches.*

Rapscallion SW4

75 Venn St   7787 6555   10–2D

This small (some say cramped) restaurant/bar opposite Clapham Picture House offers a range of wine and cocktails (and imported beers), mainly to a local crowd. It can get very crowded and noisy, but those who like the place really go a bundle on its buzzy atmosphere. / Website: www.therapscallion.co.uk **Details:** *Sun-Wed 10.30am-midnight, Thu 10.30am-1am, Fri & Sat 10.30am-2am.* **Food:** *till 11pm.*

Red W1

5 Kingly St   7434 3417   3–2C

Quite a classic of the local bar scene, this cool two-floor space was a key cocktail destination long before this part of Soho became the hipsters' haven it is today. Perhaps in keeping, it has a following which — by the standards of the area at least — is quite mature. / Website: www.redsoho.com **Details:** *Mon-Tue noon-midnight, Wed-Fri noon-1am, Sat 5pm-1am, closed Sun.* **Food:** *till 11.30pm.* **DJ:** *Fri & Sat.*

The Red Lion SW1

23 Crown Pas   7930 4141   3–4D

With its cute location in a narrow St James's alleyway, this ancient boozer (which claims its 350-year-old licence is the second-oldest in the West End) looks every bit the quaint 'Olde English Pub'. Rather than tourists, though, its small and comfortable interior is generally packed with local workers, supping a pint of Adnams or Stella. Evenings can be quite a crush (but are more the time to sample the large selection of whiskies). / Details: Mon-Sat 11am-11pm, closed Sun. **Food:** *sandwiches during opening hrs.*

The Refinery SE1

110 Southwark St   468 0186   9–4B

This large and welcoming new warehouse-style bar/restaurant has been an instant hit. It can't have anything to do with the styling or the food — both of which are pretty standard — so perhaps it's simply because it's the biggest and most prominent operation in the emerging zone behind Tate Modern. / Website: www.therefinerybar.co.uk **Details:** *Mon-Wed noon-11pm, Thu & Fri noon-1am, closed Sat & Sun.* **Food:** *till 10pm.*

Retro Bar WC2

2 George Ct   7839 8760   4–4D

An offbeat location – in a small, anonymous alleyway down some steep steps off the Strand – adds to the quirky appeal of this popular, gay-friendly bar. It's well-named for its styling, although the overall effect is attractively cosy rather than being OTT. The prominent jukebox is a key feature. / **Details:** *Mon-Fri noon-11pm, Sat 5pm-11pm, Sun 5pm-10.30pm.* **Food:** *Mon-Sat noon-10pm, Sun noon-9pm.* **DJ:** *Thu.*

Rivoli Bar
Ritz Hotel W1

150 Piccadilly   7493 8181   3–3C

The Ritz's cocktail bar – removed, nowadays, from its much more evocative former location, off the Palm Court – is expensively decorated in a colourful '20s style that may take a few more decades to mellow in properly. It's clearly a smart spot for a martini, but as yet has failed to establish itself as a real destination, and on our last visit the staff's professionalism left something to be desired. Jacket and tie de rigueur. / **Website:** *www.theritzlondon.com* **Details:** *Mon-Sat 1130am-midnight, Sun noon-10pm .* **Food:** *till 10pm.*

The Rivington Grill EC2

28-30 Rivington St   7729 7053   9–1D

Half a decade on, this cool Shoreditch joint has become a 'classic' local destination. (The proprietors – also owners of the Caprice and Ivy restaurants – know a bit about classics.) Roughly half the space is given over to a comfortably understated bar, and the rest to a brasserie area serving up good British staples. / **Website:** *www.rivingtongrill.co.uk* **Details:** *Mon-Sat noon-1am, Sun noon-11pm.* **Food:** *till 11pm.*

The Roadhouse WC2

The Piazza, Covent Garden   7240 6001   4–3D

Both the name and Covent Garden location hint that this big '50s-theme basement – run by the Maxwell's group, of burger fame – is not exactly the last word in sophistication. It does have two prime virtues though: good deals at happy hour, and late opening. / **Website:** *www.roadhouse.co.uk* **Details:** *Mon-Sat 5.30pm-3am, Sun 5.30pm-midnight.* **Food:** *till 11pm.* **DJ & Live music:** *nightly.* **Happy hour:** *5.30pm-7.30pm.* **Cover charge may apply.**

Rocket W1

4-6 Lancashire Ct   7629 2889   3–2B

It may be hidden away in a cobbled mews, off Bond Street, but don't expect this bar to be anything remotely approaching a secret. On almost any weekday evening, it's packed with post-office drinkers hell bent on having a good time – and, come rain or shine, the two small rooms regularly spill out on to the courtyard. The first-floor pizza restaurant offers tasty tucker at keen prices (for this part of town), so booking is always advisable. / **Website:** www.rocketrestaurants.co.uk **Details:** Mon-Sat noon-11pm, closed Sun. **Food:** till 10pm.

Rockwell
Trafalgar Hotel SW1

2 Spring Gdns   7870 2900   2–3C

Much of the ground floor of this West End design hotel (a Hilton in disguise) is given over to the bar, and it works pretty well as a chilled space to laze around in. They've made bourbon the house speciality, and there are over a hundred types on offer. In summer, you can also drink up on the sixth storey – see Roof Garden. / **Website:** www.thetrafalgar.com/rockwell_bar.shtml **Details:** Mon-Sat 11am-1am, Sun 11am-10.30pm. **Food:** till 11pm. **DJ:** Tue-Sat. **Cover charge may apply.**

The Roof Garden
Trafalgar Hotel SW1

2 Spring Gdns   7870 2900   2–3C

It's not always open to the public – so check ahead – but if you're looking for a classy and interesting place for a summer sundowner it's well worth seeking out this design-hotel roof terrace on Trafalgar Square. Enjoy your champagne or martini as you look out on the extraordinary jumble of roads and rooftops which make up central London. / **Website:** www.trafalgar.hilton.com **Details:** Mon-Fri 5pm-11pm, Sat 2.30pm-11pm, closed Sun.

The Royal Exchange Grand Café
The Royal Exchange EC3

Cornhill   7618 2480   9–2C

Thanks to its Grade I listing, the lofty courtyard of this beautiful building in the heart of the City is preserved from redevelopment, and therefore available for use as a bar and brasserie. There are cosier spaces to drink in London, but none more elegant architecturally. If you don't want food, head for loungy bars at mezzanine level. At ground level, there is an attractive seafood bar. / **Website:** www.danddlondon.com **Details:** Mon-Fri 8am-11pm, closed Sat & Sun. **Food:** till 10pm.

visit us at hardens.com

Royal Inn on the Park E9

111 Lauriston Rd   8985 3321   1–2D

*This is a great venue for summer, when you can spill out into
the large beer gardens (or even, as the name would suggest,
Victoria Park). A big wedding cake of a place by the gates
to the park, it attracts a varied crowd. Sun lunch is a big event
here – if it's too wet and windy to go outside, you can console
yourself with the eclectic selection on the jukebox.*
/ **Details:** *Mon-Sat noon-11pm, Sun noon-10.30pm; no Amex.* **Food:** *Tue-Sat
L 12.30pm-3.30pm, D 6.30pm-10pm, Sun 12.30pm-4pm.*

The Royal Oak SE1

44 Tabard St   7357 7173   9–4C

*Rarely encountered – and very good – ales by Harvey's
of Lewes make it worth seeking out this pretty Victorian pub
(with impressively carved bar), if you find yourself down
Borough way. Despite its charms, it seems to attract a mainly
local – and mainly male – crowd.* / **Details:** *Mon-Fri 11am-11.30pm,
Sat noon-11.30pm, Sun noon-6pm; no Amex.* **Food:** *L till 2.45pm, D till
9.30pm.*

Rupert Street W1

50 Rupert St   7292 7140   4–3A

*One of the more café-like bars in Soho's gay zone, this large
and colourful corner spot makes a good drop-in destination
at any time of day. By night, of course, the DJ pumps up the
volume.* / **Website:** *www.rupertstreet.com* **Details:** *Mon-Thu noon-11pm,
Fri & Sat noon-11.30pm, Sun noon-10.30pm.* **Food:** *till 10pm.* **DJ:** *nightly.*

St Pancras Grand
St Pancras International Station NW1

Pancras Rd   7870 9900   8–3C

*A perfect rendezvous for a brief encounter with a hint
of Parisian chic. They claim to have the longest champagne bar
in the world at this splendidly bizarre bar at St Pancras station
– as it stretches for much of the length of the adjacent Eurostar
platforms, that seems likely to be true! There's light food
available to complement a very considerable range
of champagnes by the bottle or glass, and humbler beverages
too.* / **Website:** *www.searcys.co.uk/stpancrasinternational*
Details: *7am-midnight.* **Food:** *till 10.30pm.*

Salt W2

82 Seymour St   7402 1155   6–1D

When it opened in 2005, this Bayswater style-bar – implausibly situated amongst kebab stops on an Edgware Road corner – made quite a splash. Nowadays its no longer as hot a property as once it was, but can still make a good place to kill off a few hours. Its claim to fame? Over 200 malts and bourbons, and pretty much every conceivable whiskey cocktail.
/ **Website:** www.saltbar.com **Details:** Mon-Sat 11am-1am,
Sun 11am-12.30pm. **Food:** always available. **DJ:** Thu-Sat. **Cover charge may apply.**

Salusbury NW6

50-52 Salusbury Rd   7328 3286   1–2B

With an atmosphere somewhere between a coffee house and a pub, this cosy, cocooning establishment makes an excellent and slightly surprising find in up-and-coming Queen's Park. Though there's a fair selection of wines, drinkers largely go for beers (such as Adnams, Fitzberger and Hoegaarden). The dining room next to the bar serves some decent Italianate food.
/ **Details:** Mon-Thu 5pm-11pm, Sun noon-11pm, Fri & Sat noon-midnight; no Amex. **Food:** till 10.15pm.

The Scarsdale W8

23a, Edwardes Sq   7937 1811   7–1D

Located in a graceful square, away from the hubbub of Kensington High Street, this is the pub with arguably the cutest location in town. It has the added benefit of an extremely pretty, if very small, front garden (and, in summer, competition for seats is cut-throat). With its roaring fire, the place also makes a good winter destination, and hearty pub grub is served. / **Details:** Mon-Sat noon-11pm, Sun noon-10.30pm . **Food:** till 10pm, Sun till 9.30pm.

Searcy's Champagne Bar Westfield W12

Arial Way   7078 7700   7–1C

If retail therapy at this west London mega-mall is proving too exhausting, you can down a refreshing glass of fizz at this shiny white bar, in the chichi heart of 'The Village'. It's actually surprisingly pleasant, all things considered, and a visit here can come a lot cheaper than those to the nearby boutiques.
/ **Website:** www.searcys.co.uk **Details:** Mon-Sat 11am-9pm, Sun 11am-6pm. **Food:** always available.

The Seven Stars WC2

53 Carey St   7242 8521   2–2D

*Owner Roxy Beaujolais has helped raise the profile of this glorious but tiny Elizabethan pub behind the Royal Courts of Justice. As the food is pretty good too, it can sometimes get very crowded. / **Details:** Mon-Fri 11am-11pm, Sat noon-11pm, Sun noon-10.30pm. **Food:** Mon-Fri noon-9.45pm, Weekends 1pm-9pm.*

Shampers W1

4 Kingly St   7437 1692   3–2D

*Piccadilly Circus is a great area to drink – as long as you're looking for tourist-hell or a place where clipboard Nazis rule. If, on the other hand, you feel like a decent bottle of vino – and perhaps a substantial plate of nourishing grub – this bubbly (and very '70s) wine bar overseen by charming owner Simon is well worth truffling out. / **Details:** Mon-Sat 11am-11pm, closed Sun . **Food:** till 11pm .*

The Sherlock Holmes WC2

10 Northumberland St   7930 2644   2–3C

What a brilliant marketing wheeze it was to give this pub – far removed from Baker Street – the name it has, which seems to have succeeded in establishing it on just about every tourist trail in town. For a central London boozer, though – near Trafalgar Square – it's a pleasant-enough spot, and it does have some interesting Holmes 'memorabilia' (and some available for you to buy too...).
*/ **Website:** www.sherlockholmespub.homestead.com **Details:** Mon-Thu 11am-11pm, Fri & Sat 11pm-midnight, Sun noon-10.30pm. **Food:** till 10pm.*

Shillibeer's N7

Carpenter's Mews, North Rd   7700 1858   8–2C

*Originally created as the garage for the world's first horse-drawn buses, this tucked-away bar inhabits the dodgy-looking no-man's-land between Holloway and Islington. If you join the young crowd prepared to brave the locale, however, it offers an atmospheric environment, with lots of worn wooden floors and exposed steel and iron work. There's also a courtyard. Thu night is student night. / **Website:** www.shillibeers.com **Details:** Mon-Wed 11am-11pm, Thu 11am-midnight, Fri & Sat 11am-2am, Sun 11am-11pm. **Food:** till 10pm.*

The Ship SW18

41 Jews Rw   8870 9667   10–2B

The charm of its riverside location may be partially offset by the proximity of one of south west London's busiest roundabouts, but this Wandsworth Young's boozer remains amazingly popular. It's a complete zoo on sunny days – when the food options are pepped up by the addition of a barbecue – but it also makes an atmospheric destination for a winter pint. / **Website:** www.theship.co.uk, www.youngs.co.uk **Details:** Sun-Wed 11am-11pm, Thu-Sat 11am-midnight . **Food:** till 10pm.

Ship & Shovell WC2

1-3 Craven Pas   7839 1311   2–3C

You'd be forgiven if you thought you were seeing double even before entering this curious pub – it's actually split into two halves, one on either side of the Arches beneath Charing Cross Station (with a bar in each half, and an underground passageway for the staff). Novelty is not the only reason for a visit, however, as there are also excellent Badger beers from Dorset. / **Details:** Mon-Sat 11am-11pm, closed Sun. **Food:** Mon-Fri noon-3.30pm, Sat noon-4pm.

Shochu Lounge W1

37 Charlotte St   7580 6464   2–1C

In the basement of the fashionable Fitzrovia Japanese restaurant, Roka (sibling to Knightsbridge's smash-hit Zuma), this richly-decorated subterranean den is named after its house speciality, bottles of which line the walls. (As you'll know, it's a kind of vodka-ish Japanese spirit, flavoured with fruits and herbs.) Ice comes Japanese-style – as chips hacked from a single block. / **Website:** www.shochulounge.com **Details:** Mon & Sat 5pm-midnight, Tue-Fri noon-midnight, Sun 6pm-midnight. **Food:** L Tue-Fri till 3.30pm, D Mon-Sat till 11.30pm, Sun till 10.30pm. **DJ:** Thu-Sat.

Simpson's of Cornhill EC3

38 1/2 Cornhill   7626 9985   9–2C

For a re-creation of Dickensian London, you couldn't better this ancient City chophouse (est. 1757), which – though it's best known as an eating place – also has a characterful, if cramped, ground floor bar. The small yard is an ideal open-air location for a lunchtime pint. / **Details:** Mon-Fri 11.30am-4pm, closed Sat & Sun. **Food:** L till 3pm.

Simpsons-in-the-Strand WC2

100 Strand   7836 9112   4–3D

Best known for serving roast beef (and nowadays big breakfasts too), this famed Covent Garden institution also boasts a little-known bar – decorated in calming shades of green, with black-and-white signed photographs of 1920s stars on the walls – that's worth bearing in mind for a pre-theatre drink. / **Website:** www.simpsonsinthestrand.co.uk **Details:** Mon-Sat 11am-11pm, Sun noon-6pm. **Food:** B 7.15am-10.30am, L 12.15pm-3pm.

606 Club SW10

90 Lots Rd   7352 5953   5–4B

Especially by Chelsea standards, this atmospheric jazz dive benefits from a gritty urban location. The neighbouring power station has been decommissioned, though, and the developers are putting the area ever more on the map – visit now before the place's hidden, speakeasy charms get too discovered. NB: though a full menu is available, it's much better to eat elsewhere first! / **Website:** www.606club.co.uk **Details:** Mon-Thu 7.30pm-1am, Fri & Sat 8pm-1.30am, Sun 7pm-11pm. **Food:** till midnight. **Cover charge may apply.**

06 St Chad's Place WC1

6 St Chad's Pl   7278 3355   8–3D

In a back alley behind the King's Cross Thameslink, this stunning conversion of former industrial premises comes as a real surprise. By day (when the glazed roof comes into its own), the place is a bright café/bar/restaurant – by night, it's more of an out-and-out drinking den (and one which feels all the better for its recherché location). / **Website:** www.6stchadsplace.com **Details:** Mon-Fri 8am-11pm, closed Sat & Sun. **Food:** till 9.30pm. **DJ:** Fri.

The Slaughtered Lamb EC1

34-35 Great Sutton St   7253 1516   9–1B

It sounds like it should be some ancient tavern, but this pub in the depths of Clerkenwell was recently converted from a big, two-floor space that used to be an art gallery. With its regular live gigs (and poetry readings) it has a loungy vibe not dissimilar from other Barworks group properties, such as Soho's Two Floors or the Hoxton Square Bar & Grill. / **Website:** www.theslaughteredlambpub.com **Details:** Mon-Thu 11.30am-midnight, Fri & Sat noon-1am, Sun noon-10.30pm. **Food:** noon-11pm .

Slim Jims Liquor Store N1

112 Upper St   7354 4364   8–3D

*This recent addition to Upper Street (near Islington Green)
styles itself as 'the UK's first LA-style dive bar'. The centrepiece
of its brick-walled interior is a long bar crammed with tequilas,
malts and rums, and — when there isn't entertainment or live
music — the background is predominantly heavy rock. All in all,
the performance manages to be comforting and welcoming
rather than cheesy... just about.*
/ **Website:** www.slimjimsliquorstore.com **Details:** Mon-Wed 4pm-2am,
Thu 4pm-3am, Fri & Sat noon-3am, Sun noon-2am.

Smiths of Smithfield EC1

Smithfield Mkt   7251 7950   9–1A

*This large NYC-style warehouse conversion was an early mover
in the 'trendification' of the Smithfield Market area, and it
remains a key local hang-out. The ground floor café/bar, with its
stripped-back industrial décor, is hugely popular all week —
from post-work drinks to a legendary Sun brunch. On the next
level are the 'Wine Rooms' offering 140 bins (20 by the glass)
plus champagnes, cocktails and small food plates.*
/ **Website:** www.smithsofsmithfield.co.uk **Details:** Mon-Wed noon-midnight,
Thu-Sat 11am-12.30am, Sun noon-10.30pm. **Food:** till 5pm . **DJ:** Wed-Sat.

So.uk SW4

165 Clapham High St   7622 4004   10–2D

*No disrespect to Clapham, but it's impressive how this low-lit
and seductive bar conveys a degree of sophistication that seems
at odds with its high street location. If there is such a tribe
as the Clapham Beautiful People, this is where you'll find it,
lounging on the low sofas, and toying with Moroccan snacks.*
/ **Details:** Mon-Wed 5pm-midnight, Thu-Sat 5pm-2am, Sun 5pm-midnight.
Food: till 10pm. **DJ:** Wed-Sun.

The Social N1

33 Linton St   7636 4992   1–2C

*This duo of DJ bars (with an offshoot in Nottingham and
a record label, Heavenly) was spawned by a long-running club
night (The Heavenly Social). The branch at the top of Regent
Street is a chilled, welcoming hang-out, where the action take
place in the narrow, boothed basement bar. Islington occupies
an old tavern, and is more of a gastropub.*
/ **Website:** www.thesocial.com **Details:** Mon-Wed noon-midnight, Thu-Sat
noon-1am. **Food:** always available. **DJ:** Mon-Sat. **Live music:** Mon-Wed.
Cover charge may apply.

The Social W1

5 Little Portland St   7636 4992   3–1C

*This duo of DJ bars (with an offshoot in Nottingham and
a record label, Heavenly) was spawned by a long-running club
night (The Heavenly Social). The branch at the top of Regent
Street is a chilled, welcoming hang-out, where the action takes
place in the narrow, boothed basement bar. Islington occupies
an old tavern, and is more of a gastropub.*
/ **Website:** www.thesocial.com **Details:** Mon-Wed noon-midnight, Thu & Fri
noon-1am Sat 1pm-1am, closed Sun. **Food:** always available. **DJ:** nightly.
Live music: Mon-Tue. **Cover charge may apply.**

Somers Town Coffee Hs NW1

60 Chalton St   7691 9136   8–3C

*Many people have observed that gastropubs are, culturally
speaking, Britain's answer to the French bistro, so it's perhaps
a surprise that there are so few 'cross-over' establishments
combining a boozer's cosiness with Gallic culinary savoir-faire.
In the middle of a public housing estate, near Euston, this is
one such. Don't fret, though, they do good English beers as well
as the cuisine of La Patrie.* / **Website:** www.somerstowncoffeehouse.com
Details: Mon-Sat noon-11pm, Sun noon-10.30pm. **Food:** till 10pm.

Sosho EC2

2a Tabernacle St   7920 0701   9–1C

*A classic SOuth of SHOreditch hang-out, this comfortably-
furnished member of the excellent Match bar chain is still
popular after all these years. A varying musical diet from the
regular DJs is one part of the formula, and a cocktail menu
featuring 'modern classics' is another. The food isn't bad either.*
/ **Website:** www.sosho3am.com **Details:** Tue noon-midnight, Wed & Thu
noon-1am, Fri noon-3am, Sat 7pm-4am, Sun 9pm-6am, closed Mon. **Food:** till
10.30pm, Sat till 11pm. **DJ:** Wed-Sun. **Cover charge may apply.**

The Spaniards' Inn NW3

Spaniard's Rd   8731 8406   8–1A

*Dick Turpin, Keats and Byron — not to mention Count Dracula —
are among the historical and literary associations of this
celebrated 16th-century coaching inn, right by Hampstead
Heath. It is a fine survivor of days gone by, and its plus points
include a characterful and quite spacious interior, a large and
attractive garden, and even a car-park. It claims to be the
first pub in the world to offer an automatic dog wash, for use
after walkies on the heath.* / **Details:** Mon-Fri noon-11pm, Sat & Sun
10am-11pm. **Food:** till 10pm.

The Sporting Page SW10

6 Camera Pl   7349 0455   5–3B

Many pubs have an awning promoting a popular local tipple, and it's no different at this boozer in the heart of Chelsea, recently refurbished, where the red shades bear the single word 'Bollinger'. A pint of bitter is an equally acceptable choice, though, and the atmosphere is relaxed. At weekends, the place provides community support for locals who have inexplicably failed to get away to The Country.
*/ **Website:** www.thesportingpagechelsea.co.uk **Details:** Mon-Fri 11am-11pm, Sat noon-11pm, Sun noon-10.30pm. **Food:** Mon-Fri L 10am-3pm, D 5pm-10pm, Sat & Sun noon-9pm.*

St John's N19

91 Junction Rd   7272 1587   8–1C

*This convivial boozer offers a welcome oasis of civilisation on the edge of Archway. The star of the show is the amazing rear dining room (which was once a Victorian music hall, and where good food is now served), but the whole joint is very relaxed and civilised throughout. / **Details:** 5pm-11pm. **Food:** till 11pm, Sun till 9.30pm.*

The American Bar
Stafford Hotel SW1

16 St James's Pl   7493 0111   3–4C

*Hidden away in a very cute St James's backwater, this is the sort of classic, cosy cocktail bar of which London is all too short. It is nicely cluttered with mementoes of past customers – the ceiling comes festooned with ties, hats and the occasional cuddly toy. Many of the punters live up to the place's name, but there are plenty of locals, too. Jackets for the gents after 5pm. / **Website:** www.thestaffordhotel.co.uk **Details:** 11.30am-11pm . **Food:** always available.*

Star & Garter SW15

4 Lower Richmond Rd   8788 0345   10–1B

*Occupying the bottom of this huge riverside landmark near Putney Bridge, this spacious venue makes a nice 'plain vanilla' destination. Its large bar benefits from big picture windows that allow you fully to enjoy the view, so it makes an especially good location on a sunny day. / **Website:** www.thestarandgarter.com*
***Details:** Mon-Thu 5pm-midnight, Fri 5pm-1am, Sat noon-1am, Sun noon-10.30pm. **Food:** Mon-Thu & Sun till 10pm, Fri & Sat till 9pm.*
Cover charge may apply.

The Star Tavern SW1

6 Belgrave Mews West   7235 3019   5–1D

This Fullers pub occupies an elegant Georgian building in a hidden-away Belgravia mews. It claims its place in the history books as the site of the planning of the Great Train Robbery of 1963 (but then South Kensington's Anglesea Arms does too). A recent innovation is a full-service dining room, upstairs.
/ **Website:** www.fullers.co.uk **Details:** *Mon-Sat 11am-11pm, Sun noon-10.30pm.* **Food:** *L till 4pm, D till 9pm no food served on the weekends.*

The Stinging Nettle W12

55 Goldhawk Rd   8743 3016   7–1C

It was the Railway Tavern... then it was The Bushranger... now – having been taken over by Young's – this two-floor tavern by Goldhawk Road tube has a new name. Despite its regular rebrandings and refurbs, its appeal as an upbeat modern pub attracting a lively crowd remains a constant. There are movie and DJ nights, but the top draw is the balcony, where on a fine day you can catch the rays. / **Website:** *www.thestingingnettle.co.uk* **Details:** *noon-midnight.* **Food:** *till 10pm.*

Stone Mason's Arms W6

54 Cambridge Grove   8748 1397   7–2C

Perched on a trafficky corner of Hammersmith highway, this relaxed gastropub makes a welcome find. Nowadays owned by Fullers, it's been a consistent performer over the years, with a fair selection of wines and beers and dependable cooking. The terrace is nicer than it should be, given the location. / **Details:** *noon-11pm.* **Food:** *till 10pm, Sun till 9.30pm.*

Strongroom Bar EC2

120-124 Curtain Rd   7426 5103   9–1D

Tucked-away down an alleyway, this low-key bar – with board-games, jukebox and a monthly music quiz – is a place to head for when you just want a quiet bevvy, away from the pumping beats of many of its more happening Shoreditch neighbours (ironic really, as it's actually part of a major recording studios complex). There is food served all day, as well as an extensive list of wines, beers, malt whiskies, cocktails...
/ **Website:** *www.strongroom.com* **Details:** *9am-late; no Amex.* **Food:** *always available.* **DJ:** *varies - see website.* **Live music:** *varies-see website.*

Sun SW4

47 Old Town 7622 4980 10–2D

This funky pub is a linchpin of the Clapham social scene, especially in summer when its Old Town location and large courtyard (equipped with numerous heaters) really come into their own. There are drinks for all tastes, including cocktails and a (recently expanded) range of beers. / **Details:** Mon-Fri noon-11pm, Sat & Sun noon-1am. **Food:** till 10pm.

The Sun & 13 Cantons W1

21 Gt Pulteney St 7734 0934 3–2D

A location in the heart of Soho helps explain the surprisingly hip following for this stylish but still quite traditional boozer (named, apparently, in honour of the Swiss watchmakers who used to trade nearby). The place is hottest on Fri nights (Oct-Mar), when there's a DJ in the basement bar. / **Website:** www.fullers.co.uk **Details:** Mon-Fri noon-11pm, Sat 6pm-11pm, closed Sun. **Food:** L noon-3pm, D 7pm-10pm. **DJ:** Fri. **Cover charge may apply.**

The Sun & Doves SE5

61-63 Coldharbour Ln 7733 1525 1–4C

A funked-up boozer lacking pretensions that's long been one of Camberwell's best watering holes, thanks to its cool interior (bedecked with regularly changing art), great garden and decent grub. Large without being cavernous, it seems to attract a notably friendly crowd. (Classic) film nights too.
/ **Website:** www.sunanddoves.co.uk **Details:** Sun-Thu 11am-11pm, Fri & Sat noon-midnight. **Food:** till 10.30pm, Sun till 10pm. **DJ:** Sat. **Live music:** Sun.

The Sun Inn SW13

7 Church Rd 8876 5256 10–1A

With its rambling interior, this large hostelry opposite Barnes Green has maintained its traditional spirit. Inside it's cosy and characterful, but the place really comes into its own in summer when you can sit out on the terrace, and many people like to take their drink over the road by the duck pond. Beer-lovers take note: following a recent refurb' and upgrade there are now 26 draughts on tap! / **Details:** Sun-Wed 11am-11pm, Thu-Sat 11am-midnight. **Food:** Mon-Thu till 10pm, Fri & Sat till 11pm, Sun till 9.30pm.

SW9 SW9

11 Dorrell Pl   7738 3116   10–2D

*This bright, modern bar – in an alley off the main drag –
is worth knowing about as a retreat from the Brixton mayhem.
Cocktails and trendy lagers are popular tipples, and live music
(mostly jazz) is a regular attraction. There are some pleasant
tables outside. / **Details:** Mon-Wed & Sun 10am-11pm,
Thu 10am-11.30pm, Fri & Sat 10am-1am; no Amex. **Food:** till 9pm.
Happy hour: Mon-Fri 5pm-7pm.*

Swag & Tails SW7

10-11 Fairholt St   7584 6926   5–1C

*This picturesquely located boozer is an attractive place,
well worth remembering for a civilised Knightsbridge drink.
Food is a big part of the operation (with much of the space
being given over to the dining room), and the wine list has
aspirations well above the norm. / **Website:** www.swagandtails.com
Details: Mon-Fri 11am-11pm, closed Sat & Sun. **Food:** L till 3pm, D till
10pm.*

Sway WC2

61-65 Great Queen St   7404 6114   4–1D

*A plain but spacious Covent Garden bar – with nightclub
attached – which makes a handy choice for a glass of wine or a
cocktail. There's also a restaurant which, if you stick to the
cheaper items on the menu, makes a reasonable-value place
to fuel up before a night on the tiles. / **Website:** www.swaybar.co.uk
Details: Mon-Wed noon-midnight, Thu-Fri noon-3am, Sat 6pm-3am, closed
Sun. **Food:** till midnight. **DJ:** Thu-Sat. **Happy hour:** 5pm-8pm.
Cover charge may apply.*

Taman Gang W1

141 Park Ln   7518 3160   2–2A

*This lavishly-furnished and impressively-large basement oriental,
near Marble Arch oozes conspicuous luxury with its carved
stone, Buddhas and low lighting. Join its shiny party crowd
to knock back cocktails, wine and champagne only if you're
prepared to be oblivious to the not inconsiderable cost.
/ **Website:** www.tamangang.com **Details:** Mon-Sat 6pm-1am, closed Sun.
Food: till 1am. **DJ:** nightly.*

Tamarai WC2

167 Drury Lane   7831 9399   4–1D

*Hidden away down rambling staircases in the bowels of the
New London Theatre, this dimly-lit bar benefits from impressive
nightclub-style décor, complete with screens showing trippy lotus
flower animations. Especially by Covent Garden standards it's
an enticing space, offering quality cocktails and delicious
(if expensive) pan-Asian nibbles.* / **Website:** www.tamarai.co.uk
Details: *Mon-Thu 5.30pm-2am, Fri & Sat 5.30pm-3am.* **Food:** *till 11.30pm.*
DJ: *nightly.* **Cover charge may apply.**

The Thomas Cubitt SW1

44 Elizabeth St   7730 6060   2–4A

*Belgravia has got much trendier in the last couple of years,
thanks in part to the arrival of this attractive, woody gastropub,
which has provided the younger-scene social centre the area
used so obviously to lack – at weekends, in particular, it is
constantly thronged. There's a full restaurant upstairs, and the
food is good throughout.* / **Website:** www.thethomascubitt.co.uk
Details: *noon-11pm.* **Food:** *till 10pm.*

Three Kings of Clerkenwell EC1

7 Clerkenwell Close   7253 0483   9–1A

*Funky 3-D signage advertises the presence of this freehouse
that's nearly three centuries old – a characterful place, offering
a good range of ales and lagers, plus an unusually good
selection of spirits. It's popular with local office workers,
who often spill out on to the little lane on warm evenings.*
/ **Details:** *Mon-Sat noon-11pm, closed Sun; no credit cards.* **Food:** *Mon-Sat
noon-11pm.*

Tiger Tiger SW1

29 Haymarket   7930 1885   2–2C

*If you're on the pull, or up for a Big Night Out in the West End
(or both), make a beeline for this three-floored meat-market,
whose dine-to-disco attractions include a variety of themed
cocktail bars. Wonderful or appalling – depending entirely
on your state of mind. Expect to queue for entry.*
/ **Website:** www.tigertiger.co.uk **Details:** *Mon-Sat 11am-3am,
Sun noon-midnight.* **Food:** *till midnight, bar snacks till close.* **DJ:** *nightly.*
Happy hour: *5pm-8pm.* **Cover charge may apply.**

The Toucan W1

19 Carlisle St   7437 4123   4–2A
*A charmingly scruffy Irish boozer, off Soho Square, whose unaffected friendliness more than makes up for its lack of space. Guinness – obviously – is a speciality, accompanied by an impressive range (the largest in London, they say) of Irish whiskeys. Warm weather and Fri nights see the crowd spilling out on to the street. / **Website:** www.thetoucan.co.uk **Details:** Mon-Sat 11am-11pm, closed Sun; no Amex. **Food:** till 3pm .*

The Town of Ramsgate E1

62 Wapping High St   7481 8000   11–1A
*Less touristy than its more famous neighbour, The Prospect of Whitby, this Wapping boozer still offers plenty of history – the crew of HMS Bounty took their last drink here before setting sail – and lots of atmosphere. So expect to be joined by locals and journo's from the nearby Murdoch empire when you're supping your bitter or lager, and admiring the river views from the tiny garden. / **Details:** Mon-Sat noon-midnight, Sun noon-11pm; no Amex. **Food:** till 9pm.*

Townhouse SW3

31 Beauchamp Pl   242 1428   5–1C
*A cocktail emporium, which is indeed housed in an elegant townhouse, and which is firmly aimed at the cooler end of the Knightsbridge lounge lizard market. They certainly spent plenty of money on the modernistic décor, and the range of libations is impressive. / **Website:** www.lab-townhouse.com **Details:** Mon-Sat 4pm-midnight, Sun 4pm-11.30pm. **Food:** always available. **DJ:** nightly.*

Trader Vics W1

22 Park Ln   7493 8000   3–4A
*Elvis Presley was in the charts when this Polynesian bar opened in the basement of the new Hilton hotel in 1963. More than 40 years on, the bar – part of a chain which also has branches in the likes of Atlanta, Marbella and Dubai – may similarly be credited with 'classic' status, and if kitsch is your thing it's still hard to beat. A long and pricey list of cocktails is available, accompanied – if you must – by fairly substantial eats. / **Website:** www.tradervics.com **Details:** 5pm-1am. **Food:** till 12.30am.*

The Trafalgar Tavern SE10

Park Row   8858 2909   1–3D

This famous Regency public house nestles beside Wren's Royal Naval College at Greenwich. Downstairs, its elegantly-proportioned rooms have huge bow windows looking right over the river. Upstairs, the intriguing and ship-themed Hawke & Howe bar (not always open) is worth seeking out. Legendary names associated with the place include Dickens, and the atmosphere is absolutely in keeping. Try to eat elsewhere. / Website: www.trafalgartavern.co.uk Details: Mon-Thu noon-11pm, Fri & Sat noon-midnight, Sun noon-10.30pm ; no Amex. Food: Mon-Sat till 10pm, Sun till 4pm.

Trafik EC1

331 Old St   7613 0234   9–1D

Just off Hoxton Square, this unpretentious bar – with couches, armchairs and friendly staff – is more down-to-earth than many nearby. It fills slowly, but is usually packed by the end of the evening as it's open late and there's no cover charge. Head to the dark and dingy downstairs if you're in the mood to check out the DJ and dancefloor. / Website: www.trafikinfo.co.uk Details: Mon-Sat 5.30pm-2pm, closed Sun. Food: bar snacks. DJ: Thu-Sun. Happy hour: Mon & Tue 5.30pm-11pm, Wed & Thu 5.30pm-9pm, Fri 5.30pm-8pm.

Trailer Happiness W11

177 Portobello Rd   7727 2700   6–1B

"The e-z-boy feel of a low-rent, mid-60s California valley bachelor pad" – that's the aim of this "retro-sexual haven of cosmopolitan kitsch and faded trailer park glamour". With walls covered in huge screen prints, this basement hang-out on a Notting Hill corner does have a certain je ne sais quoi, with tiki tipples the libations of choice (there are also classic cocktails, wines and beers). / Website: www.trailerhappiness.com Details: Tue-Fri 5pm-11.30pm, Sat 7pm-midnight, Sun 6pm-10.30pm, closed Mon. Food: till 10.30pm.30. DJ: Thu-Sat.

Trinity Arms SW9

45 Trinity Gdns   7274 4544   10–2D

Sitting at one of the outside tables in this leafy and tranquil square, it's hard to remember that Brixton High Street is a mere 90 seconds' stroll away. The décor, similarly, couldn't be further apart from most of the gritty urban style bars that dominate the area. So relax, and get yourself a pint of Young's bitter. / Website: www.youngs.co.uk Details: Mon-Thu 11am-11pm, Fri & Sat 11am-midnight, Sun noon-11pm; no Amex. Food: till 10pm.

Troubadour SW5

265 Old Brompton Rd   7370 1434   5–3A

This wonderfully atmospheric Earl's Court coffee shop has been considerably expanded in recent years, but its Boho ambience has survived. It's really a café in the Continental style, busy at almost all hours. In the evenings, this leads to an ambience which – paradoxically – is rather like your classic English wine bar. The basement club – where Bob Dylan, Jimi Hendrix and Paul Simon once played – offers a programme of jazz, comedy and poetry. / **Website:** www.troubadour.co.uk **Details:** 9am-12.30am. **Food:** till 11pm. **Cover charge may apply.**

25 Canonbury Lane N1

25 Canonbury Ln   7226 0955   8–2D

A tucked-away location (in a side street off the top of Upper Street) adds to the appeal of this unusually cute Islington cocktail bar – a former pub whose interior charmingly mixes styles ancient and modern. It has recently moved to all-day opening, and now serves Thai food in the evenings. / **Website:** www.25canonburylane.co.uk **Details:** Mon-Thu noon-midnight, Fri & Sat noon-1am, Sun noon-11pm; no Amex. **Food:** till 10pm, L only Sat & Sun (1pm-6.30pm).

Two Floors W1

3 Kingly St   7439 1007   3–2D

When it opened a decade or so ago, this spacious west Soho hang-out seemed frighteningly trendy. Even if the world around has changed, this place hasn't much, and it still offers a mellow environment in which to chill out (especially, perhaps, in the downstairs Tikki Bar). / **Website:** www.twofloors.co.uk **Details:** Mon-Thu noon-11.30pm, Fri & Sat noon-midnight, closed Sun; no Amex. **Food:** till 4.30pm.

Upstairs SW2

89B Acre Ln   7733 8855   10–2D

There's something of a speakeasy feel to this wonderful Clapham bar/restaurant, which benefits from being located in an intriguing corner building, above a shop. On the top floor, there's a very good French restaurant. Below, a small but popular bar, in the Gallic style, where a wide range of whiskies is a particular attraction. / **Website:** www.upstairslondon.com **Details:** Tue-Thu 6.30pm-1am, Fri & Sat 6.30pm-3am. **Food:** Tue & Wed till 9.30pm, Thu-Sat till 10.30pm.

Vats WC1

51 Lamb's Conduit St   7242 8963   2–1D

This cosy and woody Bloomsbury wine bar is done out in a very atmospheric early-'70s style, and is a favourite of the local business and legal crowds. Owned and run for over 30 years by a husband-and-wife team, it has a large, traditional wine list (strongest in claret), and offers some quite substantial food. In summer, there are a few pavement tables. / Details: Mon-Fri noon-11pm, closed Sat & Sun. Food: L till 2.30pm, D till 9.30pm.

Vertigo 42
Tower 42 EC2

Old Broad St   7877 7842   9–2C

For an unbeatable panorama of the City, where better than the top floor champagne & seafood bar of the building once known as the NatWest Tower? As the availability of 30 varieties of bubbly hints, however, this is not a place to economise. Reservations should be made in advance.
/ Website: www.vertigo42.co.uk Details: Mon-Fri noon-3pm & 5pm-11pm, closed Sat & Sun. Food: till 9.30pm.

The Vibe Bar E1

91-95 Brick Ln   7377 2899   9–1D

A few years ago, this big hang-out – with its mismatched décor, uneven wooden flooring and graffitied walls – helped turn Brick Lane into a going-out destination rather than just somewhere to grab a late-night curry. Its fantastic courtyard area probably remains the key attraction, but its rambling interior also makes a mellow (if shabby and slightly studenty) environment for killing time. / Website: www.vibe-bar.co.uk Details: Sun-Thu 11am-11.30pm, Fri & Sat 11am-1am. DJ: nightly. Live music: Thu-Sat. Cover charge may apply.

Victoria SW14

10 West Temple   8876 4238   10–2A

To say this revamped gastropub, in a leafy backstreet, is Sheen's most stylish place is not the double-edged compliment it might seem. You just didn't get places like this distinctively decorated, rambling pub in the 'burbs a few years ago, and, with its huge dining conservatory, it remains a key destination hereabouts. New owners in 2008 seem to have maintained good standards. / Website: www.thevictoria.net Details: Mon-Sat 8.30am-11pm, Sun 11am-10pm. Food: Mon-Fri noon-10pm, Sat 3pm-10pm, Sun roast noon-8pm.

Village East SE1

171-173 Bermondsey St   7357 6082   9–4D

Bermondsey hipsters – some of whom presumably like to think they're on the fringe of NYC's East Village – have adopted this large bar/restaurant en masse, and ensure that its various levels and spaces are almost invariably buzzy and atmospheric destinations. It helps that the cocktails are pretty good, and the food's not bad either. / **Website:** www.villageeast.co.uk **Details:** Mon-Thu noon-3.30pm & 6pm-10pm, Sat noon-4pm & 6pm-10.30pm, Sun noon-4pm & 6pm-9.30pm. **Food:** Mon-Thu noon-3.30pm & 6pm-10pm, Sat noon-4pm & 6pm-10.30pm, Sun noon-4pm & 6pm-9.30pm.

Village Soho W1

81 Wardour St   7434 2124   3–2D

Having entrances on both Wardour and Brewer streets isn't the only factor giving this well-established spot something of a split personality – it's a gay bar (the biggest in Soho, they say) that also seems to attract lots of mixed couples (thanks, perhaps, to the cheap late-night drinking possibilities). DJs every night, extended happy hours, and entertainments at weekends all help create a party atmosphere. / **Website:** www.village-soho.co.uk **Details:** Mon-Sat 4pm-1am, Sun 4pm-11.30pm. **DJ:** Thu & Sat. **Live music:** Thu-Sat 11pm-midnight. **Happy hour:** till 3pm-8pm.

Vinoteca EC1

7 St John St   7253 8786   9–1B

This Smithfield "bar and wine shop" is a Mecca for those who value good vino – some 300 – at reasonable prices, with much of its appeal coming from the knowledgable advice of the enthusiastic staff. If you want to make a meal of it, very decent bistro dishes, from an open kitchen, are also available. / **Website:** www.vinoteca.co.uk **Details:** noon-11pm. **Food:** L till 3pm, D till 10pm.

Vivat Bacchus

4 Hays Ln SE1   7234 0891   9–2A
47 Farringdon St EC4   7353 2648   9–2A

South African wines are really what this welcoming multi-level Farringdon wine bar (and its new London Bridge offshoot) is all about, and account for the lion's share of the 18,000 bottles in its cellars. You can eat simple fare too, but – aside from the contents of the cheese room – it's less of an attraction. / **Website:** www.vivatbacchus.co.uk.

Volt Lounge SW1

17 Hobart Pl   7235 9696   2–4B

If you're 35+, and looking for a smart nightclub-style destination for a night out, it's worth seeking out this Belgravia joint (just a couple of minutes' walk from Victoria). It includes a number of intimate bar areas (and you can also eat here quite well, if not inexpensively). / Website: www.voltlounge.com **Details:** *Sun-Thu noon-midnight, Sat 5pm-midnight.* **Food:** *L till 3.30pm, D till 11pm.* **Cover charge may apply.**

Walmer Castle W11

58 Ledbury Rd   7229 4620   6–1B

In another postcode this might be a nicer-than-usual traditional boozer. But a location at the heart of trendy Notting Hill has made it a fave rave with hip local twenty- and thirtysomethings. Its popularity is most evident in summer, when there's a pavement-clogging crush outside its front door. Good cheap Thai scoff (served in the intimate upstairs dining room) adds to its appeal. / Website: www.walmercastle.co.uk **Details:** *Mon-Thu noon-11pm, Fri & Sat noon-midnight, Sun noon-10.30pm.* **Food:** *till 10.30pm.*

The Warrington W9

93 Warrington Cr   7592 7960   1–2B

No student of Victorian pub architecture would want to miss this monumental Maida Vale tavern, with its vast and ornate bar. Theoretically, having received a Gordon Ramsay make-over, the upstairs dining room should now be a culinary Mecca too. Sadly, though, many people preferred the place when it was a cheapo Thai, so stick to a pint of beer downstairs. / Website: www.gordonramsay.com/thewarrington **Details:** *noon-11pm.* **Food:** *bar food always available.*

The Waterway W9

54 Formosa St   7266 3557   6–1C

A few years ago, no one could have dreamt that the tatty old 'Paddington Stop' (which had a nice Little Venice location going for it, but nothing else) would one day become one of the better-looking bars in town. It combines a sleek interior with a beautiful terrace (where they do barbecues in the summer). Food is quite a big part of the operation, but it's expensive for what it is (and can be served very slowly at busy times). / Website: www.thewaterway.co.uk **Details:** *Mon-Fri noon-11pm, Sat & Sun 10.30am-11pm.* **Food:** *Mon-Fri noon-10.30pm, Sat 11.30pm-10.30pm, Sun 11.30pm-10pm.*

The Well EC1

180 St John St   7251 9363   9–1A

A classic gastropub in every respect – converted pub premises, unfussy décor, picture windows, exposed brickwork, good-quality grub and a strong local following. But there's more – this Clerkenwell stalwart also boasts a sumptuous cocktail lounge in the basement (Aquarium Bar, open Wed-Sat only), with leather panelling, and fish tanks in the walls.
*/ **Website:** www.downthewell.co.uk **Details:** Mon-Thu 11am-midnight, Fri 11am-1am, Sat 10.30am-1am, Sun 10.30am-11pm. **Food:** Mon-Fri L till 3pm, D 6pm.10.30pm, Sat & Sun L 10.30am-4pm, D 6pm-10pm. **DJ:** Wed. **Happy hour:** Mon 5pm-7pm.*

Wenlock Arms N1

26 Wenlock Rd   7608 3406   9–1C

It may not have the most 'obvious' location, ten minutes from Old Street tube, but this really nice old boozer (1835) is worth seeking out. It's garlanded with CAMRA awards, but it's not just a place for beer-anoraks – if you're contemplating a trip, check out the (much above-average) website for a fuller description than there's space for here.
*/ **Website:** www.wenlock-arms.co.uk **Details:** Sun-Thu noon-midnight, Fri & Sat noon-1am; no credit cards. **Food:** till 9pm.*

The Westbourne Tavern W2

101 Westbourne Park Villas   7221 1332   6–1B

*A great, heated terrace (fight for a space) perennially maintains this Bayswater boozer as a top posing spot for Portobello trendies, especially in summer. They also do some very decent grub, though getting hold of it will expose you further to the not-always-terribly-smiley staff. / **Details:** Mon 5pm-11pm, Tue-Sat noon-11pm, Sun noon-10.30pm. **Food:** L till 3pm, D till 10pm, Sun till 9pm.*

Whisky Mist at Zeta W1

35 Hertford St   7208 4067   3–4A

The Mayfair Hilton hotel's large, and slightly oddly proportioned, style-bar was relaunched as a club in mid-2008, at the hands of style gurus Nick House and Piers Adams. Although it is quite a place of the moment, non-members may be able to book tables, but only until 9.30pm.
*/ **Website:** www.whiskymist.com **Details:** Mon-Wed 5pm-1am, Thu-Sat 5pm-3am, closed Sun. **Food:** till 1am. **DJ:** Wed-Sat. **Cover charge may apply.***

White Cross Hotel TW9

Water Ln 8940 6844 1–4A

This large riverside Young's tavern, near Richmond Bridge, is a fine, traditional pub. In summer the small garden — complete with its own bar — comes into its own, but the rambling cosy interior also makes the place a good winter choice (especially when the real fires are burning). There's a large variety of wines by the glass and a good selection of pub grub (and the nice family room upstairs makes it an OK option with kids in tow). / **Food:** *Mon-Sat till 9.30pm, Sun from noon.*

The White Horse SW6

1-3 Parson's Gn 7736 2115 10–1B

It's easy to poke fun at the 'Sloaney Pony' — or, more particularly, its clientele — but few traditional pubs have moved with the times as effectively as this large Victorian pile on Parson's Green. The array of real ales and over 50 bottled beers is impressive, and there's an excellent selection of wines (with over 20 by the glass). There's a good food operation too, and a pleasant terrace. / **Website:** www.whitehorsesw6.com **Details:** *9.30am-midnight.* **Food:** *till 10.30pm.*

White House SW4

65 Clapham Park Rd 7498 3388 10–2D

One of the most consistent successes south of the river, this sleek bar/club brings a lot of West End cool to a somewhat unlikely Clapham location (near Sainsbury's). As well as a members' club, the design incorporates a number of nifty seating areas, including for dining, of which the highlight is the large summer roof terrace. / **Website:** www.thewhitehouselondon.co.uk **Details:** *Mon-Thu 5.30pm-2am, Fri 5.30pm-3am, Sat 5.30pm-4am, Sun 1.30pm-2am.* **Food:** *till 10pm.* **DJ:** *Thu-Sat & 2nd Wed 'Student Night'.* **Happy hour:** *Thu-Sat 5pm-late .* **Cover charge may apply.**

White Swan Pub & Dining Room EC4

108 Fetter Ln 7242 9696 9–2A

In the no-man's-land east of Chancery Lane, this gentrified tavern is part of Tom & Ed Martin's 'ETM Group' of quality gastropubs. Gastronomes head for the upstairs dining room, but there's every reason just to stick to the airy, traditional downstairs bar and mezzanine, where there's a good range of draught and bottled beers or wines (and also a superior bar menu of substantial dishes). / **Website:** www.thewhiteswanlondon.com **Details:** *Mon 11am-11pm Tue-Thu 11am-midnight, Fri 11am-1am , Sat & Sun open for private parties only.* **Food:** *L noon-3pm, D 6pm-10pm.*

William IV NW10

786 Harrow Rd   8969 5944   1–2B

Despite its unpropitious roadside location, this big Kensal Green gastropub has long been something of a 'destination' locally. If you're just looking for a pint, it's worth a visit at any time, but it's especially worth seeking out in summer, when the large courtyard-garden comes in to its own. The food – mainly tapas, plus good roasts on Sun – is also of some note.
/ **Website:** www.elparadorlondon.com/wiv **Details:** Mon-Thu noon-11pm, Fri & Sat noon-1am, Sun noon-10.30pm. **Food:** Mon-Fri noon-3.30pm, Sat 1pm-11pm, Sun noon-5pmpm, 6.30pm-9.30pm. **DJ:** Fri & Sat. **Happy hour:** Fri 5pm-8pm.

The Windmill on the Common SW4

Clapham Common Southside   8673 4578   10–2C

About as countrified as you'll find in south London, this large (going-on-cavernous) and ancient Young's pub on Clapham Common is a popular destination. There is a restaurant and hotel attached, and a huge car park too.
/ **Website:** www.youngs.co.uk **Details:** Mon-Sat 11am-midnight, Sun noon-11pm. **Food:** L till 3pm, D till 10pm, Sat till 10pm, Sun till 9pm.

Windsor Castle W1

29 Crawford Pl   7723 4371   3–1A

Royal and 'establishment' memorabilia cram every nook and cranny of this quirky pub (in one of the anonymous streets which surround Marylebone's Seymour Leisure Centre). The front door is even guarded by a life-sized sentry. Given this excess of patriotic devotion, it is somewhat surprising to find that the food on offer is in fact Thai. / **Details:** Mon-Thu 11am-11pm, Fri & Sat 11am-midnight, Sun noon-10.30pm; no Amex. **Food:** L till 3pm, D till 10pm, Sat D only, Sun all day.

The Windsor Castle W8

114 Campden Hill Rd   7243 9551   6–2B

This splendid Georgian tavern (named after its view, before other buildings got in the way) is a 'classic', and it attracts traditionalists of all ages. For the summer, there's a great walled garden, while the nooks and crannies of the ancient interior recall Dickensian times. All this, plus simple scoff and a good range of ales, bottled beers and wines.
/ **Website:** www.windsorcastlepub.co.uk **Details:** noon-11pm
. **Food:** Mon-Sat till 10pm, Sun till 9pm .

Wine Library EC3

43 Trinity Sq   7481 0415   9–3D

These bare but characterful cellars provide a convivial way of killing off an afternoon in the City. They're owned by a wine merchant, and you can consume any of the bottles available – from a considerable range – at retail price plus £3.50 corkage. Lunch here – a basic but enjoyable cheese and pâté buffet – is very popular, so book! Wine tastings on Tue-Thu evenings. / Website: www.winelibrary.co.uk Details: Mon 10am-6pm, Tue-Fri 10am-8pm, closed Sat & Sun. Food: L till 3pm.

Yard W1

57 Rupert St   7437 2652   4–3A

This relaxed gay bar is well-named – its star feature is the unusual galleried setting (converted from former stables), around a small open yard that's intriguingly hidden away bang slap in the centre of Soho. Summer is the key time to go – prepare for a crush! / Website: www.yardbar.co.uk Details: Mon-Thu 2pm-11.30pm, Fri & Sat 2pm-12.30pm, Sun 2pm-10.30pm. DJ: Fri & Sat.

York & Albany NW1

127-129 Parkway   7388 3344   8–3B

Gordon Ramsay's foray into running pubs hasn't been a resounding success, but this fantastic late-2008 make-over of a fine old Camden Town pub has been a great hit. Most reviews have naturally focussed on the ambitious dining operation (overseen by Angela Hartnett), but the glamorous bar is an attraction in itself. Huge windows, high ceilings and elegant décor create a lovely, light space in which to partake of a cocktail, or a glass of wine... or two. / Website: www.gordonramsay.com/yorkandalbany Details: Mon-Thu noon-midnight, Fri-Sat noon-12.30am, Sun noon-10.30pm. Food: till 10pm.

Zakudia SE1

2a Southwark Bridge Rd   7021 0085   9–3B

If you're looking for a suitable destination for a sundowner, this first-floor South Bank bar – with its panoramic views of St Paul's and the City – is ideal. This is a popular suits' spot after-work, but – with the arrival of the Bankside locals – the atmosphere hots up as the evening progresses. / Website: www.zakudia.com Details: Tue & Wed 5pm-11pm, Thu 5pm-midnight, Fri 5pm-2am, Sat noon-2am. Food: Sun-Wed till 10.30pm, Thu-Sat till 11.30pm. DJ: Fri & Sat.

Zander SW1

Buckingham Gate   7630 6644   2–3B

*Just off uninspiring Victoria Street, it's a surprise to find this
sophisticated, if rather '90s-minimalist, spot, whose claim
to fame is that its zinc-clad bar is one of the longest in Europe.
In some ways, not being in the most 'happening' of areas works
to its advantage – staff lack attitude, and work hard to make
the place a success. Adjacent, there's a restaurant, called Bank.
/ Website: www.bankrestaurants.com Details: Mon-Wed 11am-11pm,
Thu & Fri 11am-1am, Sat 5pm-1am. Food: till 11pm.*

Zero Degrees SE3

29-31 Montpelier Vale   8852 5619   1–4D

*It's been cosied up by an early-2009 refurbishment, but the
shiny industrial styling of this buzzy microbrewery can still come
as a bit of a surprise in sleepy old Blackheath. The striking
modern setting extends the place's appeal far beyond CAMRA
types, and the large restaurant area does a good line in wood-
fired pizzas. The best drinking options are home brews
of course – lagers and ales, plus seasonal variations including
fruit beers. / Website: www.zerodegrees-microbrewery.co.uk
Details: Mon-Sat noon-midnight, Sun noon-11.30pm. Food: till 11.30pm.
Happy hour: Mon-Fri 4pm-7pm.*

Zigfrid N1

11 Hoxton Sq   7613 1988   9–1D

*Designer Paul Daley has put his heart (and his own furniture)
into his industrial-looking venture, whose major plus is a terrace
overlooking Hoxton Square. Towards the end of the week,
and as the evening progresses, the pace becomes more
raucous, with DJs spinning a wide mix of music styles
(and there's regular live music, DJs and dancing in the
'Underbelly' below). / Website: www.zigfrid.com Details: Mon-Sat
noon-1am, Sun noon-midnight. Food: L till 3pm, D 5pm-11pm. DJ: Thu-Sun.*

Zuma SW7

5 Raphael St   7584 1010   5–1D

*Perma-tanned babes flirt with off-duty bankers at this sleek
Knightsbridge bar/restaurant, which seems to have mastered
the trick of being permanently 'in' with a glossy Euro-crowd.
The Japanese food is an arm-and-a-leg job, but you can hang
out over a (slightly) more affordable sake or cocktail, plus the
odd nibble at the bar, which is decked out in rock-and-glass
'Flintstone-chic'. / Website: www.zumarestaurant.com Details: Mon-Sat
noon-11pm, Sun noon-10.30pm. Food: bar snacks.*

INDEXES

BIG SCREEN TV

Central
Akbar *(W1)*
All Star Lanes: *all branches*
Aura *(SW1)*
Babble *(W1)*
Bar Soho *(W1)*
Bricklayers Arms *(W1)*
Bünker *(WC2)*
The Calthorpe Arms *(WC1)*
Cardinal *(SW1)*
The Clachan *(W1)*
Cross Keys *(WC2)*
De Hems *(W1)*
The Edge *(W1)*
The Freemason's Arms *(WC2)*
Freud's *(WC2)*
Heights Bar *(W1)*
Kettners *(W1)*
The Langley *(WC2)*
Lowlander *(WC2)*
Milk & Honey *(W1)*
Motcomb's *(SW1)*
The Old Coffee House *(W1)*
Plumbers Arms *(SW1)*
Tamarai *(WC2)*
Village Soho *(W1)*
Yard *(W1)*

West
All Star Lanes: *all branches*
Aragon House *(SW6)*
Big Easy *(SW3)*
Brinkley's *(SW10)*
The Britannia *(W8)*
Cactus Blue *(SW3)*
The Collection *(SW3)*
Duke on the Green *(SW6)*
Eight Bells *(SW6)*
Elk Bar *(SW6)*
The Enterprise *(SW3)*
George IV *(W4)*
Ginglik *(W12)*
Goat In Boots *(SW10)*
Henry J Beans *(SW3)*
The Hillgate Arms *(W8)*
The Old Ship *(W6)*
Paradise by Way of KG *(W10)*
Portobello Gold *(W11)*
The Sporting Page *(SW10)*
The Bushranger *(W12)*
Townhouse *(SW3)*
Troubadour *(SW5)*
Walmer Castle *(W11)*

North
Anam *(N1)*
Auld Shillelagh *(N16)*
The Bull & Last *(NW5)*
The Camden Head *(N1)*
The Chapel *(NW1)*
The Hemingford Arms *(N1)*
Ye Olde White Bear *(NW3)*

South
The Abbeville *(SW4)*
The Alma *(SW18)*
The Avalon *(SW12)*
Babel *(SW11)*
Bar Estrela *(SW8)*
The Bedford *(SW12)*
The Belle Vue *(SW4)*
Le Bouchon Bordelais *(SW11)*
Bread & Roses *(SW4)*
Bridge House *(SE1)*
Bull's Head *(SW13)*
Cafe Sol *(SW4)*
The Cricketers *(TW9)*
Crooked Billet *(SW19)*
Dogstar *(SW9)*
The Duke's Head *(SW15)*
Dulwich Wood House *(SE26)*
Eclipse: *SW19*
The Fire Stables *(SW19)*
The Fridge Bar *(SW2)*
The Garrison *(SE1)*
Grafton House *(SW4)*
Hare & Billet *(SE3)*
Holy Drinker *(SW11)*
Horse *(SE1)*
The Old Dr Butler's
   Head *(EC2)*
The Old School Yard *(SE1)*
Plan B *(SW9)*
Village East *(SE1)*
The White House *(SW4)*
Zero Degrees *(SE3)*

East
All Star Lanes: *all branches*
Bar Kick *(E1)*
The Bear *(EC1)*
The Bishop's Finger *(EC1)*
The Blind Beggar *(E1)*
Cargo *(EC2)*
City Limits *(E1)*
Cock Tavern *(EC1)*
Cockpit *(EC4)*
Devonshire Terr *(EC2)*
The Dickens Inn *(E1)*
$ *(EC1)*
1802 *(E14)*
El Vino's: *EC4*
El Vino's *(EC4)*
Filthy McNasty's *(EC1)*
5B Urban Bar *(E14)*
The Fox *(EC2)*

HAPPY HOUR

LATE LICENSE (OPEN PAST MIDNIGHT)

The Lonsdale House *(W11)*
The Notting Hill Arts
  Club *(W11)*
Opal *(SW7)*
Salt *(W2)*
606 *(SW10)*
Troubadour *(SW5)*
William IV *(NW10)*

North
The Albert & Pearl *(N1)*
Anam *(N1)*
Bar Vinyl *(NW1)*
Bartok *(NW1)*
The Black Cap *(NW1)*
Boogaloo *(N6)*
The Chapel *(N1)*
Cottons *(NW1)*
Cuba Libre *(N1)*
Elbow Room: *N1*
Electricity Showrooms *(N1)*
The Fellow *(N1)*
Gilgamesh *(NW1)*
Hope & Anchor *(N1)*
Hoxton Square Bar &
  K'n *(N1)*
Keston Lodge *(N1)*
King's Head *(N1)*
The Lock Tavern *(NW1)*
Shillibeer's *(N7)*
Slim Jims Liquor *(N1)*
Social: *all branches*
25 Canonbury Lane *(N1)*
York & Albany *(NW1)*

South
The Artesian Well *(SW8)*
The Avalon *(SW12)*
Bug *(SW2)*
Babel *(SW11)*
Bar du Musée *(SE10)*
The Belle Vue *(SW4)*
Cafe Sol *(SW4)*
Dogstar *(SW9)*
Eclipse: *all branches*
Florence *(SE24)*
The Fridge Bar *(SW2)*
The Gowlett *(SE15)*
Grafton House *(SW4)*
Lost Society *(SW8)*
Plan B *(SW9)*
Rapscallion *(SW4)*
So.uk *(SW4)*
Bar M *(SW15)*
SW9 *(SW9)*
Upstairs *(SW2)*
The White House *(SW4)*

East
Al's *(EC1)*
All Star Lanes: *all branches*
Anise *(EC2)*
Bar Kick *(E1)*
Bedroom Bar *(EC2)*
Callooh Callay *(EC2)*
Cargo *(EC2)*
Catch *(E2)*
$ *(EC1)*
Dragon Bar *(E1)*
Dreambagsjaguarshoes *(E2)*
Elbow Room: *EC2*
Ember *(EC1)*
5B Urban Bar *(E14)*
Green & Red *(E1)*
Home *(EC2)*
The Hoxton Pony *(EC2)*
The Light *(E1)*
Loungelover *(E1)*
Match: *EC1*
Mint Leaf Lounge *(EC2)*
Mother Bar *(EC1)*
93 Feet East *(E1)*
Parker McMillan *(EC1)*
Smiths of Smithfield *(EC1)*
Sosho *(EC2)*
Strongroom Bar *(EC2)*
The Vibe Bar *(E1)*
The Well *(EC1)*
White Swan *(EC4)*

LITERARY EVENTS (INCLUDING POETRY)

Central
The Green Carnation *(W1)*

West
Troubadour *(SW5)*

North
Boogaloo *(N6)*
The Spaniards' Inn *(NW3)*

South
Bread & Roses *(SW4)*

East
Filthy McNasty's *(EC1)*
Foundry *(EC2)*
The Slaughtered Lamb *(EC1)*
Three Kings of
  Clerkenwell *(EC1)*

LIVE MUSIC

Central
Ain't Nothing But Blues *(W1)*
Blue Posts *(W1)*
Boisdale *(SW1)*

Café Bohème *(W1)*
Brown's Hotel *(W1)*
Ebury *(SW1)*
The Edge *(W1)*
Floridita *(W1)*
The Green Carnation *(W1)*
Guanabara *(WC2)*
Mint Leaf *(SW1)*
Momo *(W1)*
Quaglino's *(SW1)*
The Roadhouse *(WC2)*
Social: *all branches*
Trader Vics *(W1)*
Village Soho *(W1)*

West

Aquasia Bar *(SW10)*
Big Easy *(SW3)*
The Britannia *(W8)*
The Castle *(W11)*
The Collection *(SW3)*
George IV *(W4)*
Ginglik *(W12)*
The Notting Hill Arts
   Club *(W11)*
Paradise by Way of KG *(W10)*
Pilot *(W4)*
606 *(SW10)*
Troubadour *(SW5)*

North

Anam *(N1)*
Auld Shillelagh *(N16)*
Bartok *(NW1)*
Boogaloo *(N6)*
Camino *(N1)*
The Chapel *(N1)*
The Hemingford Arms *(N1)*
Hope & Anchor *(N1)*
King's Head *(N1)*
Monkey Chews *(NW5)*
Saint Pancras Grand *(NW1)*
Slim Jims Liquor *(N1)*
Social: *all branches*
Wenlock Arms *(N1)*

South

Archduke Wine Bar *(SE1)*
Bug *(SW2)*
The Bedford *(SW12)*
The Belle Vue *(SW4)*
Bull's Head *(SW13)*
Dogstar *(SW9)*
The Duke's Head *(SW15)*
Exhibit *(SW12)*
The Fridge Bar *(SW2)*
The Gowlett *(SE15)*
Grafton House *(SW4)*
Half Moon *(SW15)*

Harrisons *(SW12)*
The Hartley *(SE1)*
The Old School Yard *(SE1)*
Plan B *(SW9)*
The Ship *(SW18)*
The Sun & Doves *(SE5)*

East

The Betsey Trotwood *(EC1)*
The Blind Beggar *(E1)*
Boisdale of Bishopsgate *(EC2)*
Booty's *(E14)*
Cafe 1001 *(E1)*
Catch *(E2)*
City Limits *(E1)*
Dove *(E8)*
Elephant Royale *(E14)*
Filthy McNasty's *(EC1)*
5B Urban Bar *(E14)*
Foundry *(EC2)*
Mother Bar *(EC1)*
93 Feet East *(E1)*
The Slaughtered Lamb *(EC1)*
Strongroom Bar *(EC2)*
The Vibe Bar *(E1)*

LOUNGE/COCKTAIL BAR (AND/OR SPIRITS A SPECIALITY)

Central

Absolut Ice Bar *(W1)*
Ain't Nothing But Blues *(W1)*
Akbar *(W1)*
Albannach *(WC2)*
All Star Lanes: *all branches*
Alloro *(W1)*
Alphabet *(W1)*
Annex 3 *(W1)*
Artesian *(W1)*
Aura *(SW1)*
The Avenue *(SW1)*
Babble *(W1)*
Bam-Bou *(W1)*
Bar Code *(W1)*
Bar Rumba *(W1)*
Bar Soho *(W1)*
The Berkeley, Blue Bar *(SW1)*
Bohème Kitchen & Bar *(W1)*
Boisdale *(SW1)*
The Botanist *(SW1)*
The Box *(WC2)*
Bradley's *(W1)*
Buddha Bar *(WC2)*
Café Bohème *(W1)*
Cecconi's *(W1)*
China Tang *(W1)*
The Cinnamon Club *(SW1)*

Zuma *(SW7)*

North
The Albert & Pearl *(N1)*
Anam *(N1)*
Bar Vinyl *(NW1)*
Bartok *(NW1)*
Boogaloo *(N6)*
Camino *(N1)*
Cottons *(NW1)*
Cuba Libre *(N1)*
Elbow Room: *all branches*
The Elk in the Woods *(N1)*
The Fellow *(N1)*
Gilgamesh *(NW1)*
Hoxton Square Bar & K'n *(N1)*
Keston Lodge *(N1)*
Monkey Chews *(NW5)*
Saint Pancras Grand *(NW1)*
Slim Jims Liquor *(N1)*
Social: *all branches*
St John's *(N19)*
25 Canonbury Lane *(N1)*
York & Albany *(NW1)*
Zigfrid *(N1)*

South
The Artesian Well *(SW8)*
Bug *(SW2)*
Babel *(SW11)*
Baltic *(SE1)*
Bar Estrela *(SW8)*
Cafe Sol *(SW4)*
Dogstar *(SW9)*
Eclipse: *all branches*
Exhibit *(SW12)*
The Fire Stables *(SW19)*
The Fridge Bar *(SW2)*
Grafton House *(SW4)*
Harrisons *(SW12)*
Holy Drinker *(SW11)*
The Loft *(SW4)*
Lost Society *(SW8)*
The Old School Yard *(SE1)*
Oxo Tower *(SE1)*
Plan B *(SW9)*
Rapscallion *(SW4)*
The Refinery *(SE1)*
So.uk *(SW4)*
Bar M *(SW15)*
SW9 *(SW9)*
Upstairs *(SW2)*
Village East *(SE1)*
The White House *(SW4)*
Zakudia *(SE1)*

East
Al's *(EC1)*

All Star Lanes: *all branches*
Anise *(EC2)*
Beach Blanket Babylon: *all branches*
Bedroom Bar *(EC2)*
The Big Chill Bar *(E1)*
Boisdale of Bishopsgate *(EC2)*
Bond's *(EC2)*
The Boundary *(E2)*
Cafe 1001 *(E1)*
Café Kick *(EC1)*
Callooh Callay *(EC2)*
Cantaloupe *(EC2)*
Cargo *(EC2)*
Catch *(E2)*
Cicada *(EC1)*
Le Coq D'Argent *(EC2)*
Devonshire Terr *(EC2)*
$ *(EC1)*
Dragon Bar *(E1)*
Dreambagsjaguarshoes *(E2)*
1802 *(E14)*
Elbow Room: *all branches*
Elephant Royale *(E14)*
Ember *(EC1)*
Favela Chic *(EC2)*
Foundry *(EC2)*
Great Eastern Dining Room *(EC2)*
Green & Red *(E1)*
The Hawksmoor *(E1)*
Home *(EC2)*
The Hoxton Grille *(EC2)*
The Hoxton Pony *(EC2)*
The Light *(E1)*
Loungelover *(E1)*
Malmaison *(EC1)*
Match: *all branches*
Mint Leaf Lounge *(EC2)*
Mother Bar *(EC1)*
19:20 *(EC1)*
93 Feet East *(E1)*
Northbank *(EC4)*
Parker McMillan *(EC1)*
Potemkin *(EC1)*
Prism *(EC3)*
The Rivington Grill Bar Deli *(EC2)*
The Royal Exchange *(EC3)*
Smiths of Smithfield *(EC1)*
Sosho *(EC2)*
Strongroom Bar *(EC2)*
Trafik *(EC1)*
Vertigo *(EC2)*
The Vibe Bar *(E1)*
The Well *(EC1)*

INDEXES

OUTSIDE TABLES

Central
Absolut Ice Bar (W1)
Alloro (W1)
The Audley (W1)
Bam-Bou (W1)
Bar des Amis du Vin (WC2)
Bar Soho (W1)
Bohème Kitchen & Bar (W1)
Boisdale (SW1)
The Botanist (SW1)
The Box (WC2)
Bricklayers Arms (W1)
Café Bohème (W1)
The Calthorpe Arms (WC1)
Cecconi's (W1)
Cross Keys (WC2)
Easton (WC1)
The Edge (W1)
The Endurance (W1)
Garlic & Shots (W1)
Gordon's Wine Bar (WC2)
The Grenadier (SW1)
Hush (W1)
The Lamb (WC1)
The Long Bar (W1)
Momo (W1)
Motcomb's (SW1)
5 Cavendish Square (W1)
The Norfolk Arms (WC1)
Oriel (SW1)
Bar Oscar (W1)
The Pantechnicon Rooms (SW1)
Plumbers Arms (SW1)
The Punch & Judy (WC2)
Page in Pimlico (SW1)
Rocket (W1)
Rockwell (SW1)
The Roof Garden (SW1)
Shampers (W1)
The Sherlock Holmes (WC2)
06 St Chad's Place (WC1)
The Stafford Hotel (SW1)
The Thomas Cubitt (SW1)
Vats (WC1)
Volt Lounge (SW1)
Windsor Castle (W1)
Yard (W1)

West
Admiral Codrington (SW3)
The Anglesea Arms (W6)
Anglesea Arms (SW7)
Aquasia Bar (SW10)
Aragon House (SW6)
The Atlas (SW6)
Beach Blanket Babylon: W11

The Bell & Crown (W4)
Bluebird (SW3)
Brinkley's (SW10)
The Builder's Arms (SW3)
The Bull's Head (W4)
Cactus Blue (SW3)
Dove (W6)
Duke on the Green (SW6)
E&O (W11)
Eight Bells (SW6)
Elephant & Castle (W8)
Elk Bar (SW6)
The Enterprise (SW3)
The Fox & Pheasant (SW10)
George IV (W4)
Goat In Boots (SW10)
Ground Floor (W11)
The Havelock Tavern (W14)
Henry J Beans (SW3)
The Hillgate Arms (W8)
Julie's Bar (W11)
The Ladbroke Arms (W11)
Montgomery Place (W11)
The Old Ship (W6)
Paradise by Way of KG (W10)
Pilot (W4)
Priory House (W14)
Queen's Head (W6)
The Scarsdale (W8)
The Sporting Page (SW10)
The Bushranger (W12)
Stone Mason's Arms (W6)
Troubadour (SW5)
Walmer Castle (W11)
The Warrington (W9)
The Waterway (W9)
The Westbourne Tavern (W2)
The White Horse (SW6)
William IV (NW10)
The Windsor Castle (W8)

North
The Albert (NW1)
The Arches (NW6)
Auld Shillelagh (N16)
Bartok (NW1)
The Black Cap (NW1)
Boogaloo (N6)
The Camden Head (N1)
Camino (N1)
The Chapel (NW1)
The Chapel (N1)
The Charles Lamb (N1)
The Clifton Hotel (NW8)
The Clissold Arms (N2)
Crown & Goose (NW1)
Cuba Libre (N1)
The Elk in the Woods (N1)

City Limits *(E1)*
Coach & Horses *(EC1)*
Le Coq D'Argent *(EC2)*
The Crown Tavern *(EC1)*
Devonshire Terr *(EC2)*
The Dickens Inn *(E1)*
$ *(EC1)*
Dove *(E8)*
The Dovetail *(EC1)*
The Eagle *(EC1)*
1802 *(E14)*
El Vino's: *EC4*
El Vino's *(EC4)*
Elephant Royale *(E14)*
Ember *(EC1)*
Favela Chic *(EC2)*
Filthy McNasty's *(EC1)*
5B Urban Bar *(E14)*
Foundry *(EC2)*
The Fox *(EC2)*
The Fox & Anchor *(EC1)*
The Grapes *(E14)*
The Gun *(E14)*
The Lamb Tavern *(EC3)*
The Light *(E1)*
Match: *EC1*
Medcalf *(EC1)*
The Morgan Arms *(E3)*
The Narrow Street *(E14)*
19:20 *(EC1)*
93 Feet East *(E1)*
Northbank *(EC4)*
Parker McMillan *(EC1)*
The Peasant *(EC1)*
The Prince Arthur *(E8)*
The Prospect Of Whitby *(E1)*
Royal Inn on the Park *(E9)*
Smiths of Smithfield *(EC1)*
Strongroom Bar *(EC2)*
The Town of Ramsgate *(E1)*
The Vibe Bar *(E1)*
Vinoteca *(EC1)*
The Well *(EC1)*

POOL/SNOOKER

West
Elbow Room: *all branches*

North
Elbow Room: *all branches*
Hope & Anchor *(N1)*
Social: *N1*

South
Anchor Tap *(SE1)*
Balham Bowls *(SW12)*
Bar Estrela *(SW8)*
Half Moon *(SW15)*

East
The Bear *(EC1)*
The Blind Beggar *(E1)*
Catch *(E2)*
El Vino's: *EC4*
Elbow Room: *all branches*
19:20 *(EC1)*
Parker McMillan *(EC1)*

QUIZ NIGHTS

Central
The Calthorpe Arms *(WC1)*
The Fox & Hounds *(SW1)*
Retro Bar *(WC2)*

West
Eight Bells *(SW6)*
Harwood Arms *(SW6)*
The Hillgate Arms *(W8)*
The Bushranger *(W12)*

North
The Albert *(NW1)*
The Bull & Last *(NW5)*
The Hemingford Arms *(N1)*
Ye Olde White Bear *(NW3)*
Slim Jims Liquor *(N1)*
Social: *N1*
Wenlock Arms *(N1)*

South
Anchor Tap *(SE1)*
The Bedford *(SW12)*
Bread & Roses *(SW4)*
The Cutty Sark Tavern *(SE10)*
Dulwich Wood House *(SE26)*
Half Moon *(SW15)*
Hare & Billet *(SE3)*
The Mayflower *(SE16)*
The Ship *(SW18)*
Sun *(SW4)*
The Sun & Doves *(SE5)*

East
The Approach Tavern *(E2)*
The Blind Beggar *(E1)*
Cantaloupe *(EC2)*
Cat & Mutton *(E8)*
City Limits *(E1)*
Dreambagsjaguarshoes *(E2)*
Royal Inn on the Park *(E9)*
The Slaughtered Lamb *(EC1)*
Strongroom Bar *(EC2)*
Three Kings of
   Clerkenwell *(EC1)*

REAL FIRE

Central
The Albert *(SW1)*

The Settle Inn *(SW11)*
Sun *(SW4)*
The Sun Inn *(SW13)*
Upstairs *(SW2)*
Victoria *(SW14)*
White Cross Hotel *(TW9)*
The Windmill on the
    Common *(SW4)*

East

The Approach Tavern *(E2)*
Beach Blanket
    Babylon: *all branches*
Bleeding Heart *(EC1)*
The Blind Beggar *(E1)*
Cicada *(EC1)*
City Limits *(E1)*
Dove *(E8)*
Dreambagsjaguarshoes *(E2)*
The Fox *(EC2)*
The Fox & Anchor *(EC1)*
The Golden Heart *(E1)*
The Grapes *(E14)*
Great Eastern Dining
    Room *(EC2)*
The Gun *(E14)*
The Jerusalem Tavern *(EC1)*
Malmaison *(EC1)*
Mother Bar *(EC1)*
Ye Olde Cheshire
    Cheese *(EC4)*
Ye Olde Mitre Tavern *(EC1)*
The Peasant *(EC1)*
The Prospect Of Whitby *(E1)*
The Punch Tavern *(EC4)*
Royal Inn on the Park *(E9)*
Three Kings of
    Clerkenwell *(EC1)*

TABLE FOOTBALL

West
Cross Keys *(SW3)*
George IV *(W4)*

North
Hope & Anchor *(N1)*

East
Bar Kick *(E1)*
Café Kick *(EC1)*

TRADITIONAL PUB
(AND/OR BEER A
SPECIALITY)

Central
The Albert *(SW1)*
Argyll Arms *(W1)*
The Audley *(W1)*

Blue Posts *(W1)*
Bricklayers Arms *(W1)*
Bünker *(WC2)*
The Calthorpe Arms *(WC1)*
Cardinal *(SW1)*
The Chandos *(WC2)*
The Cittie of Yorke *(WC1)*
The Clachan *(W1)*
The Coach & Horses *(W1)*
The Coal Hole *(WC2)*
The Couch *(W1)*
Cross Keys *(WC2)*
De Hems *(W1)*
The Dog & Duck *(W1)*
Dover Castle *(W1)*
Easton *(WC1)*
The Edgar Wallace *(WC2)*
The Endurance *(W1)*
The Fox & Hounds *(SW1)*
The Freemason's Arms *(WC2)*
French House *(W1)*
The Grenadier *(SW1)*
The Guinea *(W1)*
Jugged Hare *(SW1)*
The Lamb *(WC1)*
The Lamb & Flag *(WC2)*
Lowlander *(WC2)*
The Museum Tavern *(WC1)*
The Nag's Head *(SW1)*
Nordic *(W1)*
The Norfolk Arms *(WC1)*
The Old Coffee House *(W1)*
Plumbers Arms *(SW1)*
The Punch & Judy *(WC2)*
Page in Pimlico *(SW1)*
The Red Lion *(SW1)*
The Seven Stars *(WC2)*
The Sherlock Holmes *(WC2)*
Ship & Shovell *(WC2)*
The Star Tavern *(SW1)*
The Sun & 13 Cantons *(W1)*
The Thomas Cubitt *(SW1)*
The Toucan *(W1)*
Windsor Castle *(W1)*

West
Admiral Codrington *(SW3)*
The Anglesea Arms *(W6)*
Anglesea Arms *(SW7)*
The Antelope *(SW1)*
Aragon House *(SW6)*
The Atlas *(SW6)*
The Bell & Crown *(W4)*
Big Easy *(SW3)*
The Britannia *(W8)*
The Builder's Arms *(SW3)*
The Bull's Head *(W4)*
Churchill Arms *(W8)*

WINE BAR (AND/OR WINE A SPECIALITY)

MAPS

MAP I – LONDON OVERVIEW

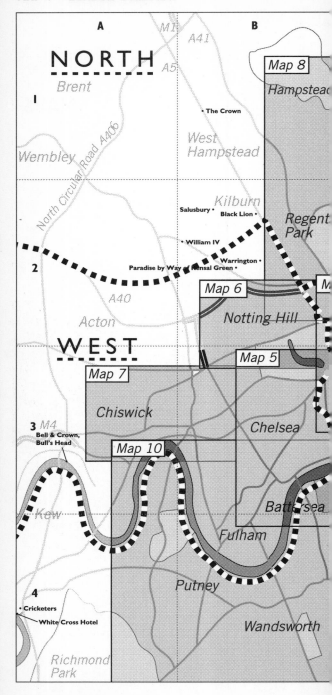

MAP 1 – LONDON OVERVIEW

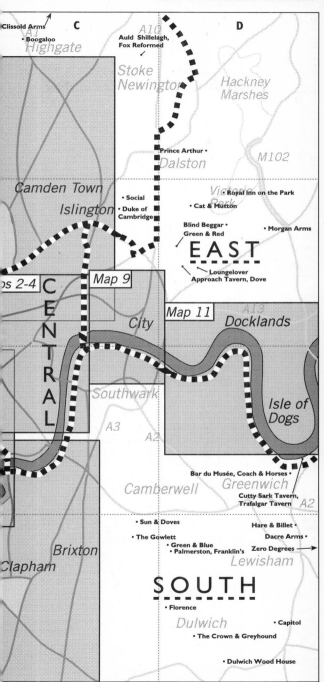

Clissold Arms
• Boogaloo
A1
Highgate

C

A10
Auld Shillelagh,
Fox Reformed

D

Stoke Newington

Hackney Marshes

M102

Prince Arthur •
Dalston

Camden Town
Islington

• Social
• Duke of
Cambridge

Victoria Park
• Royal Inn on the Park

• Cat & Mutton

Blind Beggar •
Green & Red

• Morgan Arms

E A S T

Loungelover
Approach Tavern, Dove

os 2-4 **C**

Map 9

E
N
T
R
A
L

City

Map 11

A13

Docklands

Southwark

A3

A2

Isle of Dogs

Bar du Musée, Coach & Horses •
Greenwich

Cutty Sark Tavern,
Trafalgar Tavern
A2

Camberwell

• Sun & Doves

• The Gowlett

• Green & Blue
• Palmerston, Franklin's

Hare & Billet •

Dacre Arms •

Zero Degrees

Lewisham

Brixton

Clapham

S O U T H

• Florence

Dulwich

• Capitol

• The Crown & Greyhound

• Dulwich Wood House

MAP 2 – WEST END OVERVIEW

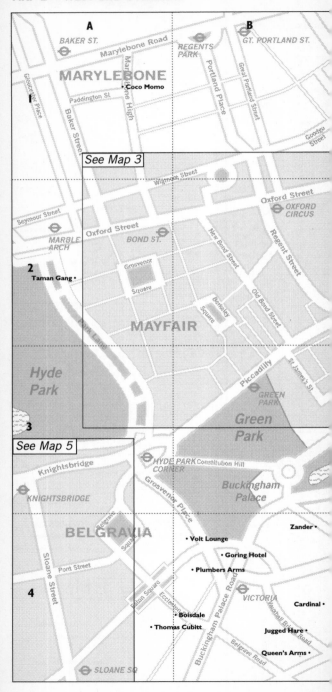

MAP 2 – WEST END OVERVIEW

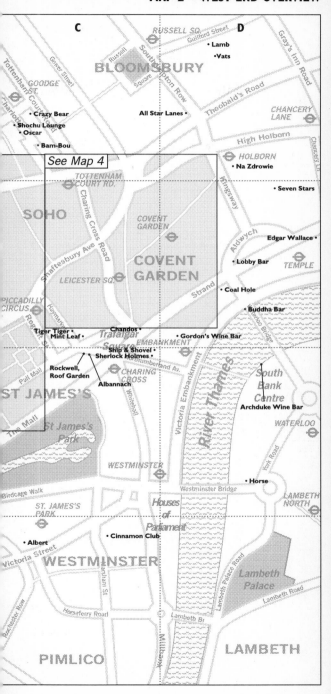

MAP 3 – MAYFAIR, ST JAMES'S & WEST SOHO

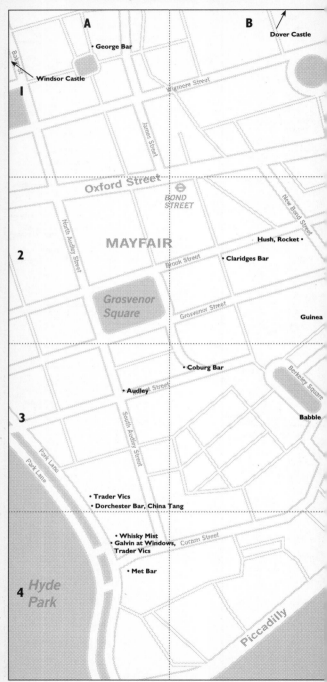

A

B

Dover Castle

• George Bar

Windsor Castle

Wigmore Street

1

James Street

Oxford Street

BOND STREET

New Bond Street

North Audley Street

MAYFAIR

Hush, Rocket •

2

Brook Street

• Claridges Bar

Grosvenor Square

Grosvenor Street

Guinea

• Coburg Bar

• Audley Street

Berkeley Square

South Audley Street

3

Babble

Park Lane

Park Lane

• Trader Vics

• Dorchester Bar, China Tang

• Whisky Mist
• Galvin at Windows,
Trader Vics

Curzon Street

• Met Bar

4 Hyde Park

Piccadilly

MAP 3 — MAYFAIR, ST JAMES'S & WEST SOHO

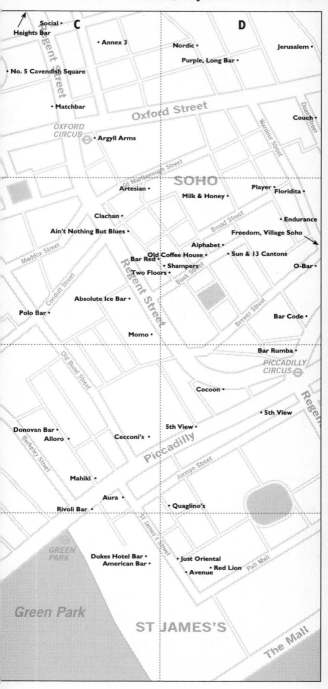

Social •
Heights Bar •

C

• Annex 3

Nordic •

Purple, Long Bar •

Jerusalem •

D

• No. 5 Cavendish Square

• Matchbar

Oxford Street

OXFORD CIRCUS

Couch •

• Argyll Arms

Gt Marlborough Street

SOHO

Artesian •

Milk & Honey •

Player • Floridita •

Clachan •

Ain't Nothing But Blues •

• Endurance

Freedom, Village Soho

Broad Street

Alphabet •

Old Coffee House •

Sun & 13 Cantons

Bar Red •

• Shampers

Two Floors •

O-Bar •

Regent Street

Beak Street

Maddox Street

Absolute Ice Bar •

Brewer Street

Polo Bar •

Conduit Street

Momo •

Bar Code •

Bar Rumba •

PICCADILLY CIRCUS

Cocoon •

Regent Street

• 5th View

Donovan Bar •

Alloro •

Cecconi's •

5th View •

Piccadilly

Berkeley Street

Mahiki •

Jermyn Street

Aura •

Rivoli Bar •

• Quaglino's

St James's Street

GREEN PARK

Dukes Hotel Bar •

American Bar •

• Just Oriental

• Red Lion

• Avenue

Pall Mall

Green Park

ST JAMES'S

The Mall

MAP 4 – EAST SOHO, CHINATOWN & COVENT GARDEN

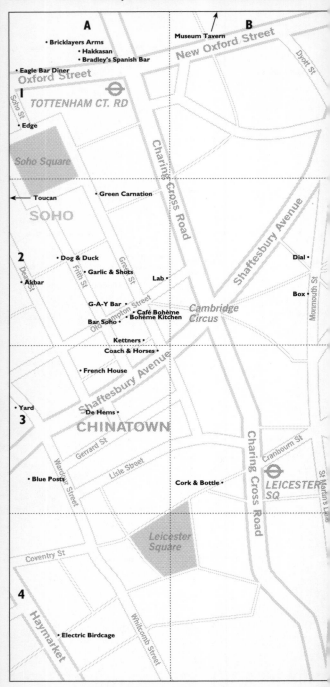

MAP 4 – EAST SOHO, CHINATOWN & COVENT GARDEN

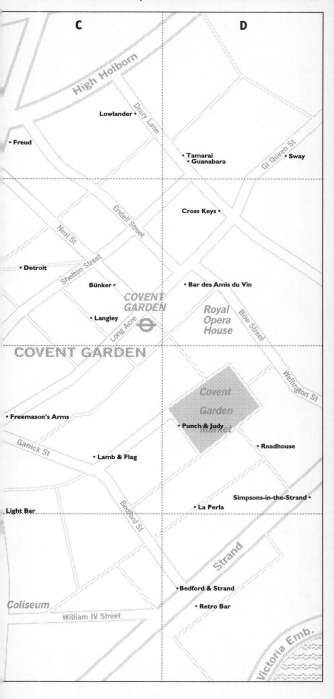

MAP 5 – KNIGHTSBRIDGE, CHELSEA & SOUTH KENSINGTON

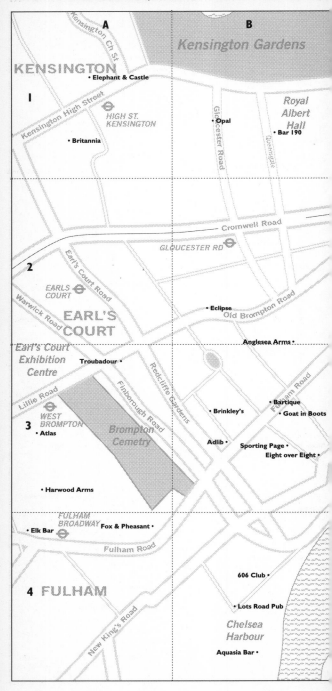

MAP 5 – KNIGHTSBRIDGE, CHELSEA & SOUTH KENSINGTON

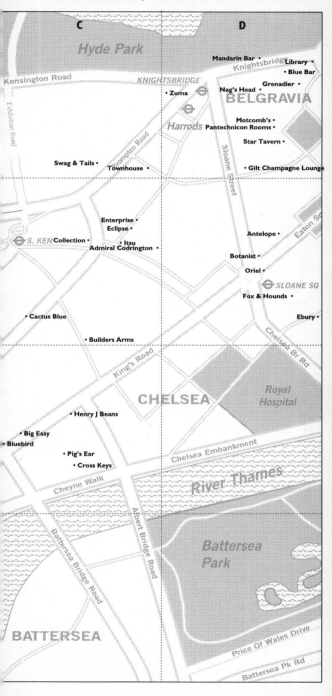

C

D

Hyde Park

Kensington Road

KNIGHTSBRIDGE

Mandarin Bar •

Knightsbridge

Library •

• Blue Bar

Grenadier •

Nag's Head •

BELGRAVIA

• Zuma

Harrods

Motcomb's •

Pantechnicon Rooms •

Star Tavern •

Exhibition Road

Brompton Road

Swag & Tails •

• Townhouse •

• Gilt Champagne Lounge

Sloane Street

Eaton Sq

Enterprise •

Eclipse •

S. KEN Collection •

• Itsu

Admiral Codrington •

Antelope •

Botanist •

Oriel •

SLOANE SQ

Fox & Hounds •

• Cactus Blue

Ebury •

• Builders Arms

Chelsea Br Rd

King's Road

CHELSEA

Royal Hospital

• Henry J Beans

• Big Easy

Bluebird

Chelsea Embankment

• Pig's Ear

• Cross Keys

Cheyne Walk

River Thames

Battersea Bridge Road

Albert Bridge Road

Battersea Park

BATTERSEA

Price Of Wales Drive

Battersea Pk Rd

MAP 6 – NOTTING HILL & BAYSWATER

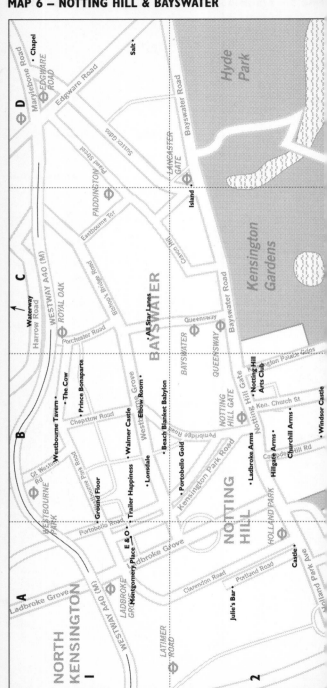

MAP 6 – NOTTING HILL & BAYSWATER

Hyde Park

Kensington Gardens

NORTH KENSINGTON

BAYSWATER

NOTTING HILL

Chapel
Salt
Waterway
The Cow
Prince Bonaparte
Westbourne Tavern
Walmer Castle
West Elbow Room
Beach Blanket Babylon
Ground Floor
Trailer Happiness
Lonsdale
Portobello Gold
E & O
Montgomery Place
All Star Lanes
Island
Notting Hill Arts Club
Ladbroke Arms
Hillgate Arms
Churchill Arms
Windsor Castle
Castle
Julie's Bar

Ladbroke Grove
Edgware Road
Marylebone Road
Bayswater Road
Queensway
Bishop's Bridge Road
Harrow Road
Porchester Road
Westbourne Park Road
Chepstow Road
Pembroke Road
Kensington Park Road
Portobello Road
Ladbroke Grove
Clarendon Road
Portland Road
Holland Park Ave

MAP 7 – HAMMERSMITH & CHISWICK

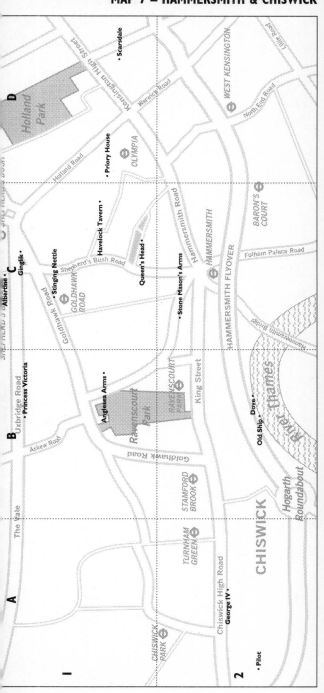

MAP 8 – HAMPSTEAD, CAMDEN TOWN & ISLINGTON

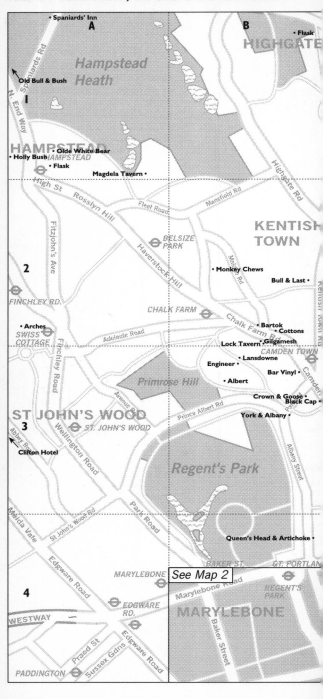

• Spaniards' Inn

A

B

• Flask

HIGHGATE

Hampstead Heath

N End Way

Old Bull & Bush

I

Highgate Rd

HAMPSTEAD

Olde White Bear

• Holly Bush   HAMPSTEAD

• Flask

Magdela Tavern •

High St

Rosslyn Hill

Fitzjohn's Ave

Fleet Road

Mansfield Rd

KENTISH
TOWN

*BELSIZE
PARK*

Haverstock Hill

• Monkey Chews

Bull & Last •

Maiden Rd

2

FINCHLEY RD.

CHALK FARM

Chalk Farm Rd

• Bartok
  • Cottons

SWISS
COTTAGE

• Arches

Adelaide Road

Lock Tavern • •Gilgamesh

CAMDEN TOWN

Finchley Road

• Lansdowne

Engineer •

Bar Vinyl •

Primrose Hill

• Albert

Crown & Goose
          Black Cap •

ST JOHN'S WOOD

Avenue Rd

Prince Albert Rd

York & Albany •

Albany Street

3

ST. JOHN'S WOOD

Wellington Road

Abbey Rd

Clifton Hotel

Park Road

Regent's Park

Maida Vale

St John's Wood Rd

Edgware Road

Queen's Head & Artichoke •

BAKER ST.   GT. PORTLAN

MARYLEBONE

See Map 2

REGENT'S
PARK

4

Marylebone Road

EDGWARE
RD.

MARYLEBONE

WESTWAY

Praed St

Edgware Road

Sussex Gdns

Baker Street

PADDINGTON

MAP 8 – HAMPSTEAD, CAMDEN TOWN & ISLINGTON

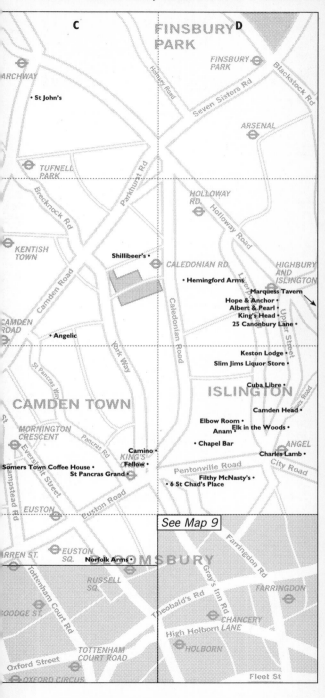

C

D

FINSBURY PARK

ARCHWAY

FINSBURY PARK

Hornsey Road

Blackstock Rd

Seven Sisters Rd

• St John's

ARSENAL

TUFNELL PARK

Brecknock Rd

Parkhurst Rd

HOLLOWAY RD.

Holloway Road

KENTISH TOWN

Camden Road

Shillibeer's •

CALEDONIAN RD.

HIGHBURY AND ISLINGTON

• Hemingford Arms

Marquess Tavern

Hope & Anchor •
Albert & Pearl •
King's Head •
25 Canonbury Lane •

Upper Street

CAMDEN ROAD

• Angelic

Caledonian Road

York Way

St Pancras Way

Keston Lodge •

Slim Jims Liquor Store •

Cuba Libre •

ISLINGTON

Camden Head •

CAMDEN TOWN

MORNINGTON CRESCENT

Pancras Rd

Elbow Room •
Anam •

Elk in the Woods •

ANGEL

Everatt Street

Camino •

KING'S

Fellow •

• Chapel Bar

Charles Lamb •

City Road

Somers Town Coffee House •
St Pancras Grand •

Pentonville Road

Hampstead Rd

EUSTON

Euston Road

Filthy McNasty's •
• 6 St Chad's Place

See Map 9

Farringdon Rd

WARREN ST.

EUSTON SQ.

Norfolk Arms •

BLOOMSBURY

Gray's Inn Rd

RUSSELL SQ.

FARRINGDON

Tottenham Court Rd

Theobald's Rd

GOODGE ST.

CHANCERY LANE

High Holborn

HOLBORN

Oxford Street

TOTTENHAM COURT ROAD

OXFORD CIRCUS

Fleet St

MAP 9 – THE CITY

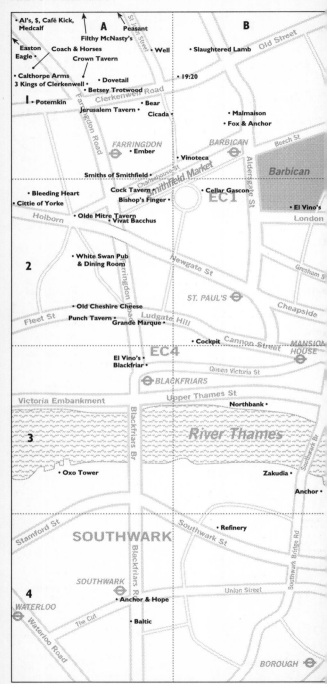

A

B

- Al's, $, Café Kick, Medcalf
- Peasant
- Filthy McNasty's
- Easton
- Eagle •
- Coach & Horses
- Crown Tavern
- • Well
- • Slaughtered Lamb
- • Calthorpe Arms
- 3 Kings of Clerkenwell
- • Dovetail
- • 19:20
- • Betsey Trotwood
- • Potemkin
- Jerusalem Tavern •
- • Bear
- • Cicada
- • Malmaison
- • Fox & Anchor

FARRINGDON
- • Ember
- • Vinoteca
- BARBICAN
- **Barbican**
- Smiths of Smithfield •
- Cock Tavern •
- Bishop's Finger •
- • Cellar Gascon
- **EC1**
- • El Vino's
- London

- • Bleeding Heart
- • Cittie of Yorke
- • Olde Mitre Tavern •
- Vivat Bacchus

2
- • White Swan Pub
  & Dining Room
- Newgate St

- **ST. PAUL'S**
- Cheapside

- • Old Cheshire Cheese
- Punch Tavern •
- Fleet St
- • Grande Marque
- Ludgate Hill
- • Cockpit
- Cannon Street
- **MANSION HOUSE**

- El Vino's •
- Blackfriar •
- **EC4**
- Queen Victoria St
- **BLACKFRIARS**

- Victoria Embankment
- Upper Thames St
- Northbank •

3
- *River Thames*

- • Oxo Tower
- Zakudia •
- **Anchor** •

- **SOUTHWARK**
- • Refinery
- Southwark St

- Stamford St

- *SOUTHWARK*
4
- *WATERLOO*
- • Anchor & Hope
- Union Street
- The Cut
- • Baltic
- Waterloo Road
- **BOROUGH**

MAP 9 – THE CITY

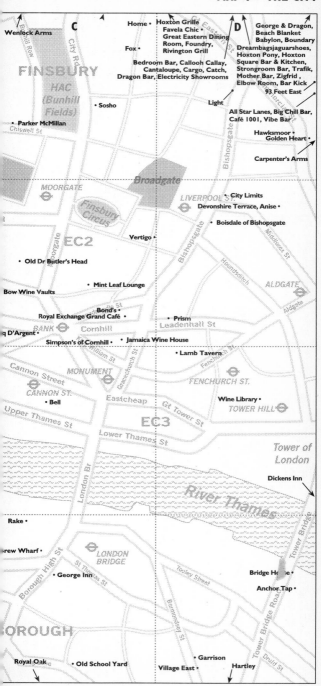

C

Wenlock Arms

Home •   Hoxton Grille
Favela Chic •
Great Eastern Dining
Room, Foundry,
Rivington Grill

Fox •

Bedroom Bar, Calooh Callay,
Cantaloupe, Cargo, Catch,
Dragon Bar, Electricity Showrooms

FINSBURY

HAC
(Bunhill
Fields)

• Sosho

• Parker McMillan

Chiswell St

D

George & Dragon,
Beach Blanket
Babylon, Boundary
Dreambagsjaguarshoes,
Hoxton Pony, Hoxton
Square Bar & Kitchen,
Strongroom Bar, Trafik,
Mother Bar, Zigfrid,
Elbow Room, Bar Kick

Light •

93 Feet East

All Star Lanes, Big Chill Bar,
Café 1001, Vibe Bar

Hawksmoor •
Golden Heart •

Carpenter's Arms

MOORGATE

Broadgate

LIVERPOOL ST • City Limits
Devonshire Terrace, Anise •

Finsbury
Circus

Vertigo •

• Boisdale of Bishopsgate

EC2

• Old Dr Butler's Head

Bow Wine Vaults

• Mint Leaf Lounge

ALDGATE

Houndsditch

Bond's
Royal Exchange Grand Café •

q D'Argent •

BANK

Cornhill

• Simpson's of Cornhill

• Prism

Leadenhall St

• Jamaica Wine House

• Lamb Tavern

MONUMENT

FENCHURCH ST.

CANNON ST.

Eastcheap

• Bell

Cannon Street

Gt Tower St

EC3

Wine Library •
TOWER HILL

Upper Thames St

Lower Thames St

Tower of
London

River Thames

Dickens Inn

Rake •

London Br

LONDON
BRIDGE

rew Wharf •

• George Inn

St Thomas St

Borough High St

ROUGH

Royal Oak •

• Old School Yard

Tooley Street

Bridge He se •

Anchor Tap •

Bermondsey St

Tower Bridge Road

Tower Bridge

• Garrison

Village East •

Hartley

Druid St

MAP 10 – SOUTH LONDON (& FULHAM)

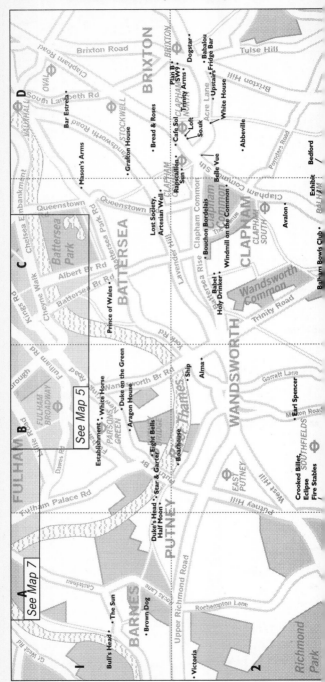

MAP 11 – EAST END & DOCKLANDS

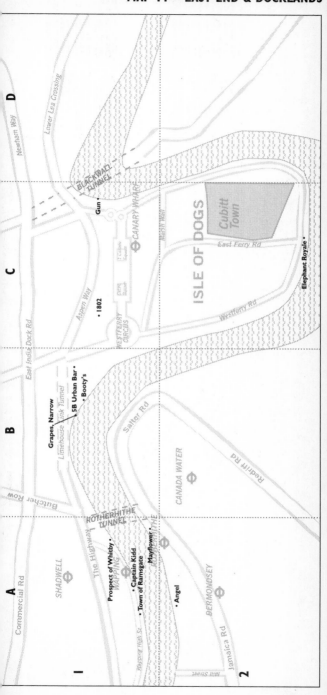